B   ...   .
          ...   .ts
unt...   ol
unt...   ...t
of te...ching ... ...years working on *Drum* maga...ine
as a journalist were to follow. An unsuccessful marriage,
together with involvement in the trial of a friend, led her to
apply for a teaching post in Botswana. Her precarious refugee
status lasted fifteen years until she was granted Botswanan
citizenship in 1979.

Her first novel, *When Rain Clouds Gather* (1969), grew out
of her experience as a refugee living at the Bamangwato
Development Farm, and was followed by *Maru* (1971) and
A Question of Power (1974). In 1977 she published *The Collector
of Treasures*, a book of short stories exploring the position of
women in Africa. In 1981 *Serowe: Village of the Rain Wind*
was published, a portrait of a village brought together from
notes and interviews spanning a hundred years. Bessie Head
died in Serowe, Botswana in 1986, aged only 49.

BESSIE HEAD

A QUESTION OF POWER

HEINEMANN

Heinemann is an imprint of Pearson Education Limited a
company incorporated in England and Wales, having its registered
office at Edinburgh Gate, Harlow, Essex, CM20 2JE.
Registered company number: 872828

www.pearson.co.za

Heinemann is a registered trademark of Pearson Education Limited

First published by Davis-Poynter Ltd, 1974
First published in the African Writers Series as AWS 149, in 1974

British Library Cataloguing in Publication Data

Head, Bessie
A question of power. (African writers series; 149)
I. Title   II. Series
823[F]   PR9408.B553H4

ISBN : 978 0 435907 20 4

For
Randolph Vigne and Christine Hawes
Ken and Myrna Mackenzie
And for Bosele Sianana,
with love

Only man can fall from God
Only man.
That awful and sickening endless, sinking
sinking through the slow, corruptive
levels of disintegrative knowledge . . .
the awful katabolism into the abyss!

D. H. LAWRENCE: From a poem: 'God'

PART ONE

SELLO

IT seemed almost incidental that he was African. So vast had his inner perceptions grown over the years that he preferred an identification with mankind to an identification with a particular environment. And yet, as an African, he seemed to have made one of the most perfect statements: 'I am just anyone'. It was as though his soul was a jigsaw; one more piece being put into place. How often was a learner dependent on his society for his soul-evolution? But then how often was a society at fault and conclusions were drawn, at the end of each life in opposition to the social trends. It wasn't as though his society were not evil too, but nowhere else could he have acquired the kind of humility which made him feel, within, totally unimportant, totally free from his own personal poisons – pride and arrogance and egoism of the soul. It had always been like this, for him – a hunger after the things of the soul, in which other preoccupations were submerged; they were intuitions mostly of what is right, but the confirmation was so strong this time that a quiet and permanent joy filled his heart. A man might laugh at intense suffering only if the evil which tortured him became irrelevant and if obsessive love, which was also one of his evils, became irrelevant too. Had it? Again, he could only apply intuition. Everything felt right with him. A barrier of solitude and bleak, arid barrenness of soul had broken down. He loved each particle of earth around him, the everyday event of sunrise, the people and animals of the village of Motabeng; perhaps his love included the whole universe. He said to himself that evening: 'I might have died before I found this freedom of heart.' That was another perfect statement, to him – love was freedom of heart.

The man's name was Sello. A woman in the village of Motabeng paralleled his inner development. Most of what applied to Sello applied to her, because they were twin souls with closely-linked destinies and the same capacity to submerge other preoccupations in a pursuit after the things of the soul. It was an insane pursuit this time. It did not bear comparing with the lofty statements of mankind's great teachers. Hidden in all their realizations were indistinct statements about evil. They never personified it, in vivid detail, within themselves. What they did say, vaguely, was that it was advisable to overcome one's passions as the source of all evil. It was harder to disclose the subtle balances of powers between people – how easy it was for people with soft shuffling, loosely-knit personalities to be preyed upon by dominant, powerful persons. The woman had at first possessed the arrogance of innocence, and had grown over a period of four years to despise the man Sello. He had freely disclosed some unpleasant and horrific details about his inner life, which damned him as a monumental sinner in her eyes. But once her relationship with the man, Dan Molomo, could be looked at with clear, hard eyes, she had turned again to Sello and held out her hands and said: 'Thank you! Oh God, thank you for the lever out of hell!' He said something in reply like: 'You see, you are just the same'. It seemed as though, now, she spent hours and hours undoing the links which bound her to Dan, whereas at one time it had been a fierce, forever relationship with wonderful music and fantastic thrills and sensations. If Dan hadn't been such a hard spitter (he spat with glorious contempt at things he dominated) she might have permanently made excuses for the other side of his song. As it was, she said: 'I might have died under the illusion that I loved him'.

The woman's name was Elizabeth. Unlike Sello and Elizabeth, the man Dan did not hold conversations with death. Only he did not look so pretty these days, and he was an extremely pretty man. It was arguable whom he wanted to destroy most, Elizabeth or Sello. The three of them had shared the strange journey into hell and kept close emotional tabs on each other. There seemed to be a mutual agreement in the beginning that an examination of inner hells was meant to end all hells forever. The pivot of the examination was Elizabeth. Both men flung unpleasant details at her in sustained ferocity. She had no time to examine her own hell. Suddenly, in one sharp, short leap to freedom, she called it Dan. He was taken off guard. He had been standing in front of her, his pants down, as usual, flaying his powerful penis in the air and saying: 'Look, I'm going to show you how I sleep with B . . . She has a womb I can't forget. When I go with a woman I go for one hour. You can't do that. You haven't got a vagina. . . .' He was going on like that when she had landed, after four years of it, on unvolcanic ground. She was shaking her head slowly, befuddled by the tablets prescribed for a mental breakdown, when suddenly Sello said something: 'Love isn't like that. Love is two people mutually feeding each other, not one living on the soul of the other, like a ghoul.' These were the first words that sank into her pain-torn consciousness after a long interval of contemptuous hatred of Sello. First she repeated the words over and over. Next, she threw the tablets out of the window. In the early morning, she sped down a dusty road, greeting any passer-by with an exuberant shout of joy. So infectious was her happiness that they responded with spontaneous smiles. The panic-stricken Dan pulled up his pants too late. He said: 'Look, I'm uplifted, I'm changed.' She no longer heard.

When Elizabeth looked back she could see that the whole story had its beginnings with Sello. The course and direction of it did not remain in his hands for long. It was taken over by Dan, first as a subtle, unseen shadow in the background, later as a wild display of wreckage and destruction. Admittedly, it had taken her a year of slow, painful thought to say at the end of it: 'Phew! What a load of rubbish!' Dan understood the mechanics of power. From his gestures, he clearly thought he had a wilting puppet in his hands. Once sure of that, he never cared a damn what he thought and did. Was it a deliberate ruse to arouse him to a total exposure? Because after she came back from the mental hospital he dropped any pose he had formally had of the great romantic lover and protector, and said: 'You are now going to have eight love affairs. You are going to be so loose your legs are going to go like this.' And he moved his large, splaying hands with lewd gestures in her face. Nothing happened. He tried another prophecy: 'You are going to commit suicide at a quarter to one tomorrow.' She nearly did, except that her small boy had asked her to buy him a football and he came down the road with a gang of eager friends. They set up a football pitch outside the house. Her son was so eager to impress everyone that he kept on kicking the football too high in the air and falling flat on his back. She spent the whole afternoon at the window watching him, he was so comical. So Dan tried another prophecy. He said: 'I have the power to take the life of your son. He will be dead in two days.' The next morning her son awoke with a high fever. Panic stricken, she rushed him to hospital. The doctor said: 'Oh, he'll be all right in a few days. You'll be more careful in future about the sores he gets when he falls down. This one on his knee has festered badly and is the cause of the fever.' The prophecies became worse and worse. Naked women were prancing wildly in front of her and there was Dan, gyrating his awful penis like mad. She swallowed six bottles of beer and six sleeping tablets to induce a blackout. She had a clear sensation of living right inside a stinking toilet; she was so broken, so shattered, she hadn't even the energy to raise one hand. How had she fallen in there? How had she fallen so low? It was a state below animal, below living and so dark and forlorn no loneliness and misery could be its equivalent. She half raised herself from the bed, intending to make a cup of tea, when Sello said quite loudly: 'I've never seen such savage cruelty'. She turned her head towards the chair where he had always sat, was it three years or four years, a ghostly, persistent commentator on all her thoughts, perceptions and experiences. Then he added: 'Love isn't like that. Love is two people mutually feeding each other. . . .'

The nightmare was over. Dan was not over. He had not yet told the whole of mankind about his ambitions, like Hitler and Napoleon, to rule the world. He had told half the story to Elizabeth. But who was she? Again she turned for her answers to Sello. She would never have earned a second glance from a man like Dan. She was not his type – Miss Glamour, Miss Beauty Queen, Miss Legs, Miss Buttocks (he said there were seventy-one of them) were all his. What concerned her was Sello and his relationship to Sello. It was Sello and what he saw in people. First, he had introduced his own soul, so softly like a heaven of completeness and perfection. Elizabeth had put tentative questions to many people, testing her sanity against theirs.

'What would you do one day if you saw someone who looked like God?' she had asked.

'Oh,' the person she spoke to had replied. 'I should love the person, but the love would be of a special quality.'

'So you think it's quite all right to start an argument from God downwards?' she asked.

'Of course you can,' he said, smiling.

Of course you can, he'd said. He was a young IVS volunteer from England. He was not African, and an argument had been worked out, in Elizabeth's mind, in an entirely African way. Perhaps in India they would have started the argument from the Superman and his accompaniment of prophecies. Nothing else need be said. In fact, they might even be hostile to any criticisms of their Gods or Supermen. If there had been a Sello in India, would the poor of India have had the courage to challenge him? Types like Sello were always Brahmins or Rama there.

One might propose an argument then, with the barriers of the normal, conventional and sane all broken down, like a swimmer taking a rough journey on wild seas. It was in Botswana where, mentally, the normal and the abnormal blended completely in Elizabeth's mind. It was manageable to a certain point because of Elizabeth's background and the freedom and flexibility with which she had brought herself up. Was the story of her mother sheer accident or design? It seemed to add to her temperament and capacity to endure the excruciating. They had kept the story of her real mother shrouded in secrecy until she was thirteen. She had loved another woman as her mother, who was also part African, part English, like Elizabeth. She had been paid to care for Elizabeth, but on the death of her husband she resorted to selling beer as a means of livelihood. It was during the war, and the beer-house mainly catered for soldiers off duty. They came along with their prostitutes and there was an awful roar and commotion going on all day. Though Elizabeth loved the woman, she was secretly relieved to be taken away from the beer-house and sent to a mission school, as hours and hours of her childhood had been spent sitting under a lamp-post near her house, crying because everyone was drunk and there was no food, no one to think about children.

The principal of the mission school was a tall, thin, gaunt, incredibly cruel woman. She was the last, possibly, of the kind who had heard 'the call' from Jesus and come out to save the heathen. Their calls seemed to make them very bitter at the end of it, and their professed love for Jesus never awakened love and compassion in their hearts. As soon as Elizabeth arrived at the mission school, she was called to one side by the principal and given the most astounding information. She said:

'We have a full docket on you. You must be very careful. Your mother was insane. If you're not careful you'll get insane just like your mother. Your mother was a white woman. They had to lock her up, as she was having a child by the stable boy, who was a native.'

Elizabeth started to cry, through sheer nervous shock. The details of life and oppression in South Africa had hardly taken form in her mind. The information was almost meaningless to her. She had always thought of herself as the child of the woman who had been paid to care for her. Seeing her tears, the gaunt missionary unbent a little, in her version of tenderness.

'There now,' she said. 'Don't cry. Your mother was a good woman who thought about you.' She stopped and rummaged among the papers, then read: 'Please set aside some money for my child's education. . . .'

It was a letter written by Elizabeth's mother from a mental hospital in South Africa. Still, she could not relate it to herself in any way. She really belonged emotionally to her foster-mother, and the story was an imposition on her life. Not so for the missionary. She lived on the alert for Elizabeth's insanity. Once Elizabeth struck a child during a quarrel, and the missionary ordered:

'Isolate her from the other children for a week.'

The other children soon noticed something unusual about Elizabeth's isolation periods. They could fight and scratch and bite each other, but if she did likewise she was locked up. They took to kicking at her with deliberate malice as she sat in a corner reading a book. None of the prefects would listen to her side of the story.

'Come on,' they said. 'The principal said you must be locked up.'

At the time, she had merely hated the principal with a black, deep bitter rage. But later, when she became aware of subconscious appeals to share love, to share suffering, she wondered if the persecution had been so much the outcome of the principal's twisted version of life as the silent appeal of her dead mother:

'Now you know. Do you think I can bear the stigma of insanity alone? Share it with me.'

Seven years later, when she had become a primary-school teacher, she returned to the small town where her foster-mother lived and said: 'Tell me about my mother.'

The foster-mother looked at Elizabeth for some time, then abruptly burst into tears.

'It's such a sad story,' she said. 'It caused so much trouble and the family was frightened by the behaviour of the grandmother. My husband worked on the child welfare committee, and your case came up again and again. First they received you from the mental hospital and sent you to a nursing-home. A day later you were returned because you did not look white. They sent you to a Boer family. A week later you were returned. The women on the committee said: "What can we do with this child? Its mother is white." My husband came home that night and asked me to take you. I agreed. The next thing was, the family came down in a car from Johannesburg on their way to the racecourse in Durban. The brother of your mother came in. He was very angry and said: "We want to wash our hands of this business. We want to forget it, but the old lady insists on seeing the child. We had to please her. We are going to leave her here for a while and pick her up later." The old lady came down every time they entered horses in the races. She was the only one who wanted to see your mother and you. When you were six years old we heard that your mother had suddenly killed herself in the mental home. The grandmother brought all her toys and and dolls to you.'

It was such a beautiful story, the story of the grandmother, her defiance, her insistence on filial ties in a country where people were not people at all. The last thing Elizabeth did in that small town where she had been born was to walk to the mental hospital and stare at it. There was a very high wall surrounding the building, and the atmosphere was so silent there hardly seemed to be people alive behind it. People had named the building the Red House because its roof was painted red. As a small child she had often walked past it. It was on the same road that led to the bird sanctuary, the favourite playground of all the children of the town. She remembered saying: 'Now we are passing the Red House,' never dreaming that her own life was so closely linked to its life. She seemed to have that element of the sudden, the startling, the explosive detail in her destiny and, for a long time, an abounding sense of humour to go with it.

For a few years she quietly lived on the edge of South Africa's life. It was interesting. She spent some time living with Asian families, where she learnt about India and its philosophies, and some time with a German woman from whom she learned about Hitler and the Jews and the Second World War. A year before her marriage she tentatively joined a political party. It was banned two days later, and in the state of emergency which was declared she was searched along with thousands of other people, briefly arrested for having a letter about the banned party in her handbag, and involved in a court case which bewildered the judge: 'Why did you bring this letter to court?' he said severely to the policeman in charge of the case. 'Can't you read English? The two people involved in the writing of this letter are extremely critical of the behaviour of people belonging to the banned party. They are not furthering the aims of communism.' It might have been the court case which eventually made her a stateless person in Botswana.

She married a gangster just out of jail. He said he had thought deeply about life while in prison. What really made her talk to him was that he said he was interested in Buddhism, and she knew a little about it from her friendships with Asian people. It seemed perfectly all right, a week later, to marry someone interested in philosophies, especially those of India. A month later a next-door neighbour approached her and said: 'You have a strange husband. Susie was standing outside the door and called to him. He walked straight in and they went to bed. He's been doing this nearly every day now with Susie. I also once greeted him and he said: "How about a kiss?" And I said: "Bugger off." What made you marry that thing?'

Women were always complaining of being molested by her husband. Then there was also a white man who was his boy-friend. After a year she picked up the small boy and walked out of the house, never to return. She read a newspaper advertisement about teachers being needed in Botswana. She was forced to take out an exit permit, which, like her marriage, held the 'never to return' clause. She did not care. She hated the country. In spite of her inability to like or to understand political ideologies, she had also lived the back-breaking life of all black people in South Africa. It was like living with permanent nervous tension, because you did not know why white people there had to go out of their way to hate you or loathe you. They were just born that way, hating people, and a black man or woman was just born to be hated. There wasn't any kind of social evolution beyond that, there wasn't any lift to the heart, just this vehement vicious struggle between two sets of people with different looks; and, like Dan's brand of torture, it was something that could go on and on and on. Once you stared the important power-maniac in the face you saw that he never saw people, humanity, compassion, tenderness. It was as though he had a total blank spot and only saw his own power, his influence, his self. It was not a creative function. It was death. What did they gain, the power people, while they lived off other people's souls like vultures? Did they seem to themselves to be most supreme, most God-like, most wonderful, most cherished? Elizabeth felt that some of the answers lay in her experiences in Botswana. That they were uncovered through an entirely abnormal relationship with two men might not be so much due to her dubious sanity as to the strangeness of the men themselves.

Motabeng means the place of sand. It was a village remotely inland, perched on the edge of the Kalahari desert. Seemingly, the only reason for people's settlement there was a good supply of underground water. It took a stranger some time to fall in love with its harsh outlines and stark, black trees. A fellow-passenger on the train to Botswana had laughingly remarked: 'You're going to Motabeng? It's just a great big village of mud huts!' The preponderance of mud huts with their semi-grey roofs of grass thatching gave it an ashen look during the dry season. During the rainy season, Motabeng was subjected to a type of desert rain. It rained in the sky, in long streaky sheets, but the rain dried up before it reached the ground. People turned their noses towards the wind and sniffed the rain, but it was so often not likely to rain in Motabeng. Elizabeth privately renamed it: The Village of The Rain-Wind, after a poem she had read somewhere. The rhythm of its life was slow-paced, like the quiet stirring of cattle turning patient, thoughtless eyes on a new day. It seemed to Elizabeth that it took people half an hour to greet each other each day. It took so long, they said, because Motabeng was a village of relatives who married relatives, and nearly everyone had about six hundred relatives. Elizabeth had a typical greeting translated for her on her arrival. It went like this:

'Good day, Mother.'

'Good day, Mother.'

'How are you?'

'I am well. How are you?'

'I am well.'

(Here follows a brief pause to catch the breath. Everyone knows this is not the end of the story.)

'The grandmother's third daughter is ill in hospital.'

'Goodness me, are you on the way there?'

'Yes. The uncle's fourth cousin is marrying the paternal uncle's fifth daughter.'

'Dear me. Will I smell some of the wedding food?'

'That's just the trouble. The paternal uncle's fifth daughter says you won't smell it because you never invited her to your child's wedding. My friend, I did not like her speech. . . .'

Well, it could go on and on like this. People often looked at Elizabeth with a cheated air. She had been taught the greeting in Setswana up to the first five lines and had no delicious titbits of gossip to offer. A person would actually put out her hand to stay her: 'Wait a bit. Where are you hurrying to?' It was so totally new, so inconceivable, the extreme opposite of 'Hey, Kaffir, get out of the way', the sort of greeting one usually was given in South Africa. Surely there was a flow of feeling here from people to people? She made her home at first in the central part of a particular village ward. They were all relatives, and she was amazed to uncover a permanent adult game that should really have been relegated to children: 'I'll bewitch you and you'll bewitch me.' A teacher explained it to her thus: Suppose someone hated him. That person would creep into his yard at night and place a bunch of dried leaves, doctored by a witch-doctor, in front of his door. Being educated, he would merely pick up the bunch of leaves and throw them away. But the ordinary villager would straight away make off to the witch-doctor for a counter-medicine. There were so few secrets in the society – the guilty party always told someone – that revenge was swift. And yet people seemed to survive all those leaves outside their door, but not malnutrition and other ailments. As soon as these struck, they remembered the witchery. This seemed to Elizabeth the only savagely cruel side to an otherwise beautiful society. They were terror tactics people used against each other. Such a terror was to fill her mind at a later stage that she would look back on the early part of her life in Botswana and think that the personality who held her life in a death-grip must really be the master of the psychology behind witchcraft.

It was barely three months after her arrival in the village of Motabeng when her life began to pitch over from an even keel, and it remained from then onwards at a pitched-over angle. At first, she found the pitch-black darkness of the Motabeng night terrifying. She had always lived in a town, with a street light shining outside the window, so the first thing she hastened to buy was a chair on which to place a candle, beside her bed. She kept the candle burning right up to the point when she felt drowsy, then blew it out. Often she fell asleep with the candle still alight. The chair, a bed and a small table were the only pieces of furniture she had in her hut. After a while she became more accustomed to the extreme dark and quite enjoyed blowing out the light and being swallowed up by the billowing darkness. One night she had just blown out the light when she had the sudden feeling that someone had entered the room. The full impact of it seemed to come from the roof, and was so strong that she jerked up in bed. There was a swift flow of air through the room, and whatever it was moved and sat down on the chair. The chair creaked slightly. Alarmed, she swung around and lit the candle. The chair was empty. She had never seen a ghost in her life. She was not given to 'seeing' things. The world had always been two-dimensional, flat and straight with things she could see and feel.

This recurred for several nights, and she simply reasoned that whatever it was was not a danger to her life. Let it sit if it wanted to. Oh, no; whatever it was wanted to introduce itself at some stage, because one night she was lying staring at the dark when it seemed as though her head simply filled out into a large horizon. It gave her a strange feeling of things being there right inside her and yet projected at the same time at a distance away from her. She was not sure if she were awake or asleep, and often after that the dividing line between dream perceptions and waking reality was to become confused.

The form of a man totally filled the large horizon in front of her. He was sitting sideways. He had an almighty air of calm and assurance about him. He wore the soft, white, flowing robes of a monk, but in a peculiar fashion, with his shoulders slightly hunched forward, as though it were a prison garment. He stared straight at Elizabeth in a friendly way and said, in a voice of quiet affection: 'My friend.'

She stared back, not replying. Then he said: 'Will you stay here for some time?'

A sort of terror gripped her chest. The words were almost jerked out of her mouth: 'No,' she said. 'I'm going to die quite soon.' He kept quiet, except that his look changed from friendliness to seriousness. A name for the monk had instinctively formed itself in her mind. He was . . . He was . . . But it was too impossible. A wave of panic made her fling her arms into the air and take a great leap out of the bed. She paced the floor for a while, violently agitated. The abrupt encounter, the strangeness of his question and the equal strangeness of her unpremeditated reply threw her mind into a turmoil. He looked like a man she had seen about the village of Motabeng who drove a green truck, but the name she associated in her mind with the monk-robed man was that of an almost universally adored God. Then nothing else seemed about to happen, and she eventually calmed down and went to sleep. She was to find out that something would startle her like this and quieten down to an apparent normality, only to find that she had really been shaken up into accepting an entirely unnatural situation and adapting it to the flow of her life. There was only one way to explain it. The principal of a school had a teacher on his staff who was fond of brandy. He took a bottle of brandy into the toilet, intending to have a few sips. Well, he kept on taking a few sips and peeping around the door to spy out the whereabouts of the principal. Soon he became quite drunk and reversed the activity. He'd open the door, take a few sips, close the door and look for the principal in the toilet. Much the same applied to her. She began by waking up on the tail-end of absorbing conversations with the white-robed monk who sat on the chair beside her bed, and it wasn't long before the discussions became a full-time activity. The faint silvery-white outline of his robe and his face were clearly discernible to her at all times, and so overpowering was the experience at first that in the early morning, as she poured out a cup of tea, she would pour a second cup and absent-mindedly walk towards the chair and say: 'Here's a cup of tea for you,' and then jolt back to reality, shaking her head: 'Agh, I must be mad! That's just an intangible form.'

Yet he was so vividly alive! It seemed also as though he had come to stay. Nothing fascinated her more than his interest in and affection for people. Every visitor to her hut earned some comment. It was more often: 'She's a lovely woman, isn't she?' or, 'I like him for his strange ways,' and very rarely: 'I don't like him, he's too small-minded.' He never hesitated to participate in every discussion, commenting aside, and, especially when something pleased him, nodding his head. Elizabeth was a voluble talker who gesticulated wildly when she talked. If some idea excited her, she'd spring to her feet and wave her arms about. She'd often swing around to the chair and point directly at it, talking all the time and vigorously including its occupant. She always said: 'Don't sit on that chair. It has a slope which hurts the back. Have a seat on the bed'. If she were so unfortunate as to forget and totally exclude the occupant of the chair from the chatter, it would sound off with a loud 'ting'. The 'ting' went off too when particularly good points had been made. No one ever seemed to notice the clamour of the side-discussion, except, on one occasion, a young Peace-Corps volunteer from America, named Tom. (Motabeng village was full of IVS and Peace Corps, as they formed almost the entire staff of the Motabeng Secondary School.) Tom had become a permanent fixture in her life since the first day they'd met. They soon began imagining they were solving all the problems of the universe together, and it was their habit to sit for hours, heads bent, working away at deep philosophical problems. She was later to depend on Tom heavily for the return of her sanity, but that night, just as he was about to leave, he laughed and turned towards her and said: 'You're a strange woman, Elizabeth. The things *you* draw out of a man! You know, men don't really discuss the deep metaphysical profundities with women. Oh, they talk about love and things like that, but their deepest feelings they reserve for other men.'

And Sello said: 'Yes, that's right,' and off went the chair with a loud 'ting'.

Tom started and looked about the room with wide, alert eyes: 'Did you hear something?' he said quickly. 'I distinctly heard someone say "Yes, that's right" ': and he kept very still, his eyes roving curiously around the room. Elizabeth kept very quiet, too, incapable of explaining the mad state of affairs in her house. Suddenly Tom said: 'Hell, I'm tired,' and stood up and walked out. He left an echo behind him – 'but their deepest feelings they reserve for other men.' Why, yes, she thought, that was the only reasonable explanation of the relationship between Sello and her. The base of it was masculine. Right from the start, Sello had the air of one who was simply picking up the threads of a long friendship that had been briefly interrupted at some stage. It was as if he was saying: 'Do you recall this occasion when we met and worked together?' Because a spectacular array of personalities moved towards her, crowded with memories of the past. They were all Sello in his work, as the prophet of mankind. She seemed to have no distinct face of her own, her face was always turned towards Sello, whom she had adored. At least, that was her stand in the few perceptions which awakened in her. She seemed to have only been a side attachment to Sello. The nearest example she could give to it, was that of a Teacher and his favourite disciple, such as many religious men had had. There were so many impressions of Sello as this religious man that she had a feeling that he was somewhat of a gymnast concerning these things, that his past life had pervaded the whole world. The best way she could present her argument was this: Say Einstein, for instance, had, at some dim beginning of his soul, decided that science was the best profession for him. And over the centuries, throughout all his incarnations, he had worked at science, till he became expert in his chosen field. Then the same process applied to Sello. He had chosen religion. It provided as well, a tentative solution for the prophecies that appeared to have accompanied him, even here.

As Dan was later to say to her: 'He never gets born without the prophecies. They included you too.' Maybe she had made too close an identification with Sello for her own comfort and safety. Maybe he was used to all the hazards which go with these proclamations, because the fearful thing was that Dan had decided that he was a much better manager of the universe than Sello. What was eating him was that no prophecies had preceded him; and yet in some way he had gained directorship of the universe in 1910. He had a staccato way of putting it: 'Directorship since 1910.' He had the prophecies on his mind like a mania, and Elizabeth could see that his main intent was to make them backfire or make them the joke of the country. He caught on to the idea of using Elizabeth as his trigger for blowing them up, and once he was sure that she hated Sello he kept on saying: 'He's shaken up. The prophecies aren't coming true.'

She could see, at some stage, all the prophecies blowing up high into the air, but what she could not foresee was the subtle way Dan was about to blow her up with them too. She lived such an absent-minded life and had such a blind spot in matters of public or social awareness that it took time to piece the fragments of information together, in some coherent form. Definitely, as far as Batswana society was concerned, she was an out-and-out outsider and would never be *in* on *their* things. She had to look back and say to herself: 'Hey, now why did they say that, and why did they do that?'

Because, on looking back, she remembered a day when the whole population of Motabeng turned around and looked at her, quietly, with vague curiosity, almost disinterestedly: 'Well, now, something's been said. Let us examine this cow.' A few of the bolder types of villagers stepped forward, with compressed lips, and posed a few blunt questions. They usually did it when she was standing idle at the post office, waiting for the mail to be sorted. A young woman said to her at this time: 'People here are waiting for something,' smiled, bent her head and added: 'Would you like to be an important person?'

She answered the second half quite easily: 'Oh no, I'm quite all right as I am.' The word 'important' could make her hair rise up. She wasn't sure if it applied elsewhere, but she was essentially a product of the slums and hovels of South Africa. People there had an unwritten law. They hated any black person among them who was 'important'. They would say, behind the person's back: 'Oh, he thinks he's *important*', with awful scorn. She had seen too many people despised for self-importance, and it was something drilled into her: be the same as others in heart; just be a person.

The first half vaguely disturbed her, then an old woman really shattered her. After all, there were all those weird goings-on in her own house. The old woman, too, looked rather disgusted. She compressed her lips tightly, looked to one side and said darkly: 'Now tell me something. I want to know, when are you going to marry Sello?'

'What?' Elizabeth asked loudly, pretending not to have heard. 'What did you say?'

Sello was married to a large Motswana woman with strangely uncomprehending eyes. She looked as though she were just content to dress well and eat well and had a heavy, stuffed-up-with-food way of walking.

Just at this time, too, a man sidled up to her and put the most impossible question of all: 'Can you tell me something about Sello?' he said. 'He doesn't like his own nation at all. He likes *your* kind of nation.' He said 'your kind of nation' with supreme contempt. She kept silent, pretending not to know Sello at all. She screwed up her face with a puzzled frown and the man walked off.

It became clear to Elizabeth that they knew something, that they were following a story with a logical outline, much as she was. This story kept on coming out in bits, as Sello felt inclined, but of one thing she was sure. He hadn't started turning the water into wine. If he had, it would have aroused considerable hysteria. As it was, people were just following along, being shaken up now and then, as she was. As for what the prophecies actually said, she had no idea. Sello kept silent about them, but talked a great deal on all kinds of other subjects. If Dan hadn't had a mania about them, she wouldn't have known.

At first she was extremely curious about the living man, Sello, thinking that in some way he corresponded to the white-robed monk who sat on the chair in her house. To her surprise, he went to elaborate lengths to set up an impassable barrier between her and him. She once turned the corner of a building and came face to face with Sello, in conversation with a short man. She stopped and stared straight at him. He slowly averted his face. She glanced at his companion, briefly. He had pretty eyes, large, luminous, black, with a thick cluster of lashes. His eyes gave his face a wonderful expression of innocence and friendliness. He immediately bowed his head to Elizabeth in silent greeting. It was Dan. Distracted, she did not return the greeting. It was on the tip of her tongue to say to Sello: 'Why are you sitting in my house?'

That was his set pattern from the beginning, the averted head. It stood out as a deliberate gesture in a society where it was almost compulsory for people to greet each other. Perhaps she was rather relieved. Sello said some strange things about women. He said he 'killed' them. Was it sheer coincidence? There was an unpleasant sort of man who constantly waylaid Elizabeth in the village, his eyes full of meaningful glances. He always began: 'I want to tell you something about Sello,' then he'd look over his shoulder. 'I come from the same place as you, and they want to tell us we can't fight their people. I don't care. If I find a man in bed with my wife, I'll fight him. If you want to know some things about the people here, I'll tell you.' She disliked the heavy suggestiveness in his eyes, but was later very astonished when Sello referred to the matter himself: 'It's quite true. He found me in bed with his wife. I felt sorry for the man but I had to kill his wife. She was like a raging beast. She's quite harmless now.'

She had occasion to meet the woman. She was an unpleasant woman, a terrible snob and social pusher. In a village like Motabeng where no one really cared how they dressed, she dressed to the teeth just for the purpose of purchasing a piece of soap from the shop. In guarded moments she was very much the madam, in full control of all situations. She looked at Elizabeth in an unguarded moment. Her eyes were dull, flat, exhausted. She raised one hand wearily and said: 'This is a terrible country to live in. You just dry up and die inside. I feel as if I had died a long time ago.'

Sello was never explicit about this 'killing' business. He said he had 'killed' several women. He said it in an aloof, detached way, as though it were simply part of a job he was on.

Very little detail reached her about Sello, the living man, who drove a green truck about the village of Motabeng. People were fond of remarking: 'You want to know about cattle and crops? Go to Sello. He knows everything.' Sello was a crop farmer and cattle breeder.

Now and then his name cropped up in a general conversation. An IVS volunteer who regularly attended parties at his house once turned to Elizabeth and said, enthusiastically: 'There's something so lovely about Sello. I don't know quite what it is.'

Once she had been standing on a pathway talking to a young Motswana nurse of the Motabeng hospital and Sello passed by in his green truck. The girl remarked: 'I love that man.'

'Why?' Elizabeth asked, interested.

'He is a wonderful family man,' she said simply. 'He keeps order in his house.'

That was the sum total of her knowledge of the living man. In many ways, her slowly unfolding internal drama was far more absorbing and demanding than any drama she could encounter in Motabeng village. The insights, perceptions, fleeting images and impressions required more concentration, reflection and brooding than any other work she had ever undertaken. Dominating and directing the whole drama was Sello. He was a fascinating person to work with, simply because his temperament was so opposed to Elizabeth's. Her mind functioned in wild leaps and bounds, overlooking many details. He always moved three paces behind, calmly, unhurriedly, the collector of the details. Even his presentation of ideas appealed to her. They were expressed in the long-paced sentences of solitary meditation. It was as though he had thought out the whole story ahead of meeting her, because he had a way of unconsciously nodding his head while talking, as much as to say: 'I know quite a lot, but people always like to contradict me.'

His proposition was the beautiful world of the future. He was sitting at a switchboard plugging in the lines to all the beautiful people he had on call. What was presented to Elizabeth as goodness remained consistently so, to the extent that she too rapidly accepted Sello as a comfortable prop against which to lean. He turned to her once and warned her to retain her own mental independence: 'You have an analytical mind. You must analyse everything you see.' She failed to heed the warning, and the day he abruptly pulled away the prop of goodness she floundered badly in stormy and dangerous seas.

'You must have suffered a lot in South Africa,' he said, by way of introduction. 'But you are not to hate white people.'

'Why?' she asked.

'Most of the Gods are born among them,' he replied, calmly. 'Some of them come here for a while, then go away again.'

He turned his head in the direction of the Motabeng

Secondary School and suddenly put in one of his plugs. A tall big-built man wearing only short khaki pants and boots came walking along the pathway to Elizabeth's house. He stood for a moment at the door. As she turned to look at him, she sprang to her feet with an exclamation of surprise and wonder. The sun had directly transferred itself to his face and its light was flying in all directions. She heard Sello say: 'He is the Father, the Father.'

He sat down on Elizabeth's bed, picked up his right leg and flung it over his left knee and looked at Sello. He said nothing, and the expression in his eyes was difficult to define. He was laughing and happy at the same time, as though he were saying silently: 'Fancy meeting you here, Comrade.' There was a feel of restless energy about him, and like Sello he had an unconscious habit. He flung his head back like a wild horse careering across the plains with the wind full in its face, as though he couldn't endure any restraints on his freedom of thought, movement, feeling. They seemed to be easily interchangeable souls, because Sello stood up, walked straight into his person and totally disappeared. 'The Father' stared in front of him for a moment, thinking something over, then he turned to Elizabeth with a slow, proud turn of his head and added two more titles to the title already given him by Sello:

'I am the king of the Underworld,' he said. 'My other name is Wonder There.'

He paused a moment and handed Elizabeth a huge pile of papers covered with small, neat handwriting. At the top of the first page was the word: Poverty. Then he turned round and reached for some garments lying at the foot of Elizabeth's bed. They were the usual tattered, dirty rags worn by the poor man in Africa. He stood up and put them on. Then he turned to the bed again and found a crown there, exceedingly beautiful and glittering with an intense white light. He held the crown in his hands briefly, looked sideways at Elizabeth and said: 'We have worked together for a long time. This is my earnings with you. We'll work together again, but you prepare the way.' He stood up to take his leave, then paused at the door and said to her, coldly, hostilely: 'Dan is fooling around with my name.'

His last sentence was meaningless to her. She had not yet encountered Dan, at least, not his soul.

Then Sello seemed to put in the plugs all at the same time, and she found herself faced with a vast company of people. They had still, sad, fire-washed faces. The meaning of the stillness, sadness and intensity of expression did not reach her till some time later, when Sello exposed a detail of his past. It was death. It was the expression of people who had been killed and killed and killed again in one cause after another for the liberation of mankind. She thought at that time: 'Why, an absolute title has been shared. There are several hundred thousand people who are God.'

It seemed to her as though all suffering gave people and nations a powerful voice for the future and a common meeting-ground, because the types of people Sello referred to as 'the Gods' turned out on observation to be ordinary, practical, sane people, seemingly their only distinction being that they had consciously concentrated on spiritual earnings. All the push and direction was towards the equality of man in his soul, as though, if it were not fixed up there, it never would be anywhere else; and her most vivid memories were the memories of those souls who stated this with the most impact.

One night she was startled to see an Asian man walk towards her with the fiercest expression on earth. Like everyone else, he addressed her as though he knew her quite well. He had pitch-black eyes and seemed half mad, his expression was so ferocious. He was so taut and tense with energy that he walked in jerky spasms. He hissed in her face: 'You have never really made an identification with the poor and humble. This time you're going to really learn how. They are going to teach you,' and he flung his arm dramatically into the air. At this gesture, a group of people walked quietly into the room. They were the poor of Africa. Each placed one bare foot on her bed, turned sideways so that she could see that their feet were cut and bleeding. They said nothing, but an old woman out of the crowd turned to Elizabeth and said: 'Will you help us? We are a people who have suffered.' She nodded her head in silent assent.

Then they all turned and looked at Sello. Like Elizabeth,

they also saw the dazzling array of prophets which was Sello's achievement. They turned their backs on him, then suddenly one of the men turned around and pointed into the distance and said:

'You are not yet ready. Our king is standing over there. He has taken off his vesture garments.'

So unexpected was the hostility they displayed towards Sello that, sensing approaching upheaval, even disaster, Elizabeth turned towards Sello and said: 'Something terrible is going to happen.' It seemed as though her thoughts came to a full stop around the man's words. If the poor of India had seen that Sello was also their Krishna and Rama, would they have told him to take off his vesture garments and become the same as everyone else? Sello's favourite hunting-ground had been India, and she privately accused him of being the originator of the caste system, alongside his other theories on the heavens.

They next turned to Elizabeth and permanently stripped her of any vesture garments she might have acquired. They said: 'There is an evil in your relationship with Sello. He knows. He is controlling your life in the wrong way, and he does not want to give it up.'

She had seen from the beginning that she had no distinct personality, apart from Sello. For some time she had been conscious of trying to make an effort to reach up to a great height. On each occasion she had fallen back half way. There seemed to be no end to the upward ascent, but as those people spoke they all turned to look at the slow descent of a man in a monk's robe. He had his hands clasped in front of him and moved straight in the direction of Elizabeth. As he approached near she stared intently at his face. His eyelids covered his eyes, and the intensity of his concentration inwards was so great that small wave-like vibrations of light continually emanated from his face. He moved into her person, silently. Elizabeth turned and looked at Sello. He averted his face. It was Buddha, and the only face she had acquired apart from Sello. A series of pictures unfolded before her.

She found herself suddenly in conversation with a tall, thin Asian man who looked like Sello. He said of Buddha:

'He refused to live again. I had to use evil to draw him back to life again. I had work to do, and there was no one who could work with me like you can. We shared everything. He had a wife. I made a false promise to her: "If you help me to pull him down, he will be yours, forever." She agreed.'

The scenes shifted. Elizabeth stood next to a man who slightly resembled her. He held a sling in his hand. Confronting them was a monstrous woman, looming so large that Elizabeth had to strain back to see her face. She looked hideous, with teeth about six inches big. She smiled with her abnormal teeth at Elizabeth. Shining out of her eyes was the tender, blue glow of a great love. Elizabeth turned to the man at her side and said: 'David, kill her.'

The man shook his head: 'I loved her,' he said.

Suddenly, out of the monstrous woman, stepped a slenderly-built woman. She stood alone, her head bent. She threw her eyes into her own heart with such intent concentration that only the whites of her eyes were discernible. Slowly, she turned her head and looked at Elizabeth. She instantly cringed with fear.

'Why did you do it?' Elizabeth asked.

Like 'the Father' she raised a glittering crown to her head. Then she said: 'This is my earnings with you.' She pointed at Elizabeth's heart: 'I made that heart of compassion,' she said. She walked into Elizabeth's person.

The crowd of people who had watched everything pointed to the monstrous woman: 'What do you say about the blood on your hands?'

Elizabeth said: 'I killed, yes, but from that day she became a follower of the Lord.'

They turned to Sello and said: 'Give up your control of her life.'

He turned to a wall where there was a safe, opened it and took out a small box which he handed to Elizabeth. He looked at Elizabeth with intense sadness and said: 'From now onwards your comings and goings are your own affair,' then he turned aside and said in a voice full of tears: 'I can still count my treasures.'

As though stricken with sorrow at his sorrow, the crowd of people knelt down softly and bowed their heads to the ground. Elizabeth had no vesture garment left. It did not matter who had planned evil. It was always there, the plan. But deeper still was human passion. There seemed to be no safeguard against it, no nobility powerful enough to counter it, no depths to which the soul could not sink. . . . 'David wrote a letter to Joab, *and sent it by the hand of Uriah*. And he wrote in the letter, saying, Set ye Uriah in the forefront of the hottest battle and retire ye from him, that he may be smitten, and die.'

Hours passed by in brooding reflection. He had a premonition that he was going to turn the day of judgement on himself. His statements became sadder and sadder.

'Will you help me?' he said to Elizabeth. 'We have always worked out our development together. I shall die in five years' time.'

Elizabeth agreed, though she did not like being handed someone else's death date, but the next night he seemed to think his death over more carefully, because he said: 'I'll live much longer than that. I want to bring up my children.'

He looked at Elizabeth, with a sudden flash of humour.

'I'm very old, you know, in my soul. I have completed a billion cycles in my destiny. You are only two.'

He bent his head. There was an old man with a ring of sparse white hair. The huge bald patch shone like polished mahogany. She looked at a projection of herself. It was a minute image of a small girl with pitch-black hair. She wobbled unsteadily on her feet.

'There are a set of people in my age-group and a set of people in your age-group. The first group brought about dark times. We had to dream a nobler dream, and the people of that dream belong to your age-group. Everything was wrong. Everything was evil until I broke down and cried. It is when you cry, in the blackest hour of despair, that you stumble on a source of goodness. There were a few of us who cried like that. Then we said: "Send us perfection." They sent you. Then we asked: "What is perfection?" And they said: "Love".'

'Who are *they*?' she asked quickly.

'There's always someone holding the ball,' he said. 'If you

look over your shoulder you will find people with hearts more generous than yours.'

It was the kind of language she understood, that no one was the be-all and end-all of creation, that no one had the power of assertion and dominance to the exclusion of other life. It was almost a suppressed argument she was to work with all the time; that people, in their souls, were forces, energies, stars, planets, universes and all kinds of swirling magic and mystery; that at a time when this was openly perceived, the insight into their own powers had driven them mad, and they had robbed themselves of the natural grandeur of life. As Darwin had perceived in the patterns of nature: 'There is grandeur in this view of life, with its several powers, having been originally breathed into a few forms or into one; and that, whilst this planet has gone cycling on according to the fixed law of gravity, from so simple a beginning endless forms most beautiful and wonderful have been, and are being, evolved.'

She was talking to a monk who had used an unnatural establishment to express a thousand and one basic principles as the ideal life because, in the heat of living, no one had come to terms with their own powers and at the same time made allowance for the powers of others. It was as though a crossroad had been reached and that people would awaken to a knowledge of their powers, but this time in a saner world. It was later that she was to draw her own conclusions about this saner world and assert them under degraded circumstances, because other searches for eternal goodness never took into account a situation with a total lack of compassion; none of mankind's God-like figureheads recorded seeing what she saw on this nightmare soul-journey.

There were many beautiful things said at that time, because an awakening of her own powers corresponded to an awakening love of mankind. They were soon lost in the subsequent torment, but what she most clearly remembered saying was: 'Oh, what a world of love could be created!' She was entirely dependent on Sello for direction and equally helpless, like a patient on his doctor for survival, assuming that the doctor knew his job. For he turned towards her at some point and directed at her a small, clear river of light.

It had the effect, on reaching her, of setting light to some enormously explosive material. Her whole form seemed to turn into channels through which raced powerful currents of energy. He kept on switching off and adjusting the currents. It must have been for about a month, working silently, until one day her head simply exploded into a sea of pale, blue light. It was the sensation which accompanied it which was so final and absolute: Here is the end of all life. Here is nothing. It did not correspond to the energies needed for the tasks of life; making tea, cooking food for a small boy, eating washing, working. She had to struggle to live, move and breathe. It was only for one day. As she lay down that night a wide corridor opened up in her mind. Just as forms were taking shape, Sello reached forward and silently drew back a thin, dark curtain between her and the explosion of activity behind it. He kept his thumb pressed against the edge of the curtain. The most appalling roar burst forth. The overall sound of it was like the hard pounding of horses' hooves or like the bumping, grating feeling of being dragged along a stony road at a wild pace. Piercing, blood-curdling yells rent the air. The whole night long she lay awake, listening to the confusion of sound. The lives of centuries unfolded before Sello alone. At dawn, the roar subsided. He removed his thumb and the dark curtain flapped to and fro in a gentle breeze.

He bent forward slightly, lost in deep thought. Eventually he said: 'I cannot awaken you, at this stage, to these things. It's impossible anyway. You just scream in terror. They've killed you again and again under the most horrible circumstances.'

Then he said, in a small, frightened voice: 'I thought too much of myself. I am the root cause of human suffering.'

There was no warning. There was no explicit statement – here I am, with a height of goodness you cannot name; there I was, at some dim time in mankind's history, with a depth of evil you cannot name. Here I am, about to strip myself of my spectacular array of vesture garments as they said I ought to, and to show you my own abyss. There are so many terrible lessons you have to learn this time; that the title God, in its absolute all-powerful form, is a disaster to its holder, the all-seeing eye is the greatest temptation. It turns a man into a wild debaucher, a maddened and wilful persecutor of his fellow men. He said none of this. Only at times when a wild terror overcame her mind did he step in with the kinds of statements that restored her mental balance.

He quietly drew towards him a woman. She had the same simple dress, a loosely-flowing white cloth draped over her shoulders and form. Her face was upturned. Though her eyes were opened, they were abstracted like those of one who lives in a permanent trance. Her long straight black hair clung like a wet mat around her shoulders and down her back. It was almost the extreme of spirituality. She was frighteningly unapproachable. He said, quietly: 'My wife', walked towards her, lifted a lock of her black hair and cut it off with a pair of scissors. There was no further communication with this image of holiness. Then from out of himself he projected a man, his replica, except that the man was clothed in a brown suit. Out of the fainting-away woman stepped a powerfully built woman. She wore a simple, white, sleeveless dress. She was flat-chested, narrow-waisted with broad hips. She was pitch-black in colour and her long black hair flowed loosely about her. Her black eyes were large, full, powerful. She walked towards Elizabeth. She had an exciting way of walking. Her thighs rubbed against each other like the rustle of silk against silk. She stopped a few paces from Elizabeth and rose into the air. She said: 'I am greater than you in goodness.'

She turned her head to one side and carefully examined Elizabeth's face, then she said: 'What are you buying this time?'

Elizabeth replied: 'Buddha.'

She pointed to Elizabeth's right hand: 'What's that?' she asked. Elizabeth raised her hand. In it was a pale blue rosette. It was made of a warm satin material and had two streamers. Elizabeth said: 'It's the prize I have to earn in this life. It is symbolic of the brotherhood of man.'

The woman bent her head as though keeping her thoughts to herself. She walked towards Elizabeth and past her. She brushed past Elizabeth so violently, the gesture said, loudly:

'Get out of the way.' Her face had assumed a mean expression. She swung around near the man in the brown suit who looked like Sello, and looked at Elizabeth like a wild-eyed Medusa. She started shouting in a shrill, high voice: 'We don't want you here. This is my land. These are my people. We keep our things to ourselves. You keep no secrets. I can do more for the poor than you could ever do.'

Elizabeth looked at the man in the brown suit and said: 'You are making a mistake, Sello. I'm God too.' The woman unsettled her. She wasn't thinking of herself. She was thinking of the title which had already been shared. The man bared his teeth in a snarl: 'You're not God,' he said.

The sudden, unexpected development jolted her fully awake. She had been so intensely drawn inwards over a certain period that her mind dwelt entirely at this intangible level of shifting images and strange arguments. She lay quietly staring in the dark. Why was everything so pointed, so absorbingly profound? The wild-eyed Medusa was expressing the surface reality of African society. It was shut in and exclusive. It had a strong theme of power-worship running through it, and power people needed small, narrow, shut-in worlds. They never felt secure in the big, wide flexible universe where there were too many cross-currents of opposing thought. She was disturbed by the awakening conflict. Sello had introduced her directly to the soul-reality of the black man. They had stood and addressed her as soul equals. Other nations, harsh climates, high peaks of endeavour and suffering had shaped her soul. Their soul-communication to her and Sello was terribly important – that people who have suffered from the wanton cruelty of others prefer the truth at all times, no matter what it might cost them. There was a certain drill she had been through over the centuries, in the strange highways and byways taken by monks, where those statements dominated: 'You are not yet ready. Take off your vesture garments.' Her mind had clutched at it eagerly, while at the same time aware of the precarious balance – there was also the village level of life, witchcraft and all the hidden terrors of darkness. The sharp edge of it had become blurred over in most advanced societies. People had their institutions, which to a certain extent protected them from power-lusting presidents for life with the 'my people' cult. Africa had nothing, and yet, tentatively, she had been introduced to one of the most complete statements for the future a people could ever make: Be ordinary. Any assumption of greatness leads to a dog-eat-dog fight and incurs massive suffering. She did not realize it then, but the possibilities of massive suffering were being worked out in her.

At some point in her reflections she started to doze off. Suddenly, a terrible thunderbolt struck her heart. She could feel wave after wave of its power spread over her body and pass out through her feet. As the last wave died down, she simply shot up into the air. There was a quick movement from the indistinct form who forever sat on the chair beside her bed. He caught hold of her in mid-air and began stuffing her back into something that felt like a heavy dead sack. It was particularly painful to push her way into the lower half of the dead sack, and her chest area was suffocating with a roaring pain.

'Oh God, oh God,' she thought, half mad with fear. 'What's happening to me?'

The Medusa was shouting, shrill and high: 'You always wanted my power. Now you have felt it.'

What was it? The Medusa was working out things at a different level, with a Sello in a brown suit who had no contact with the Sello in the monk's robe who sat on the chair nearby; because he turned to her and said: 'I'm sorry you're so badly hurt. I couldn't pull that power out of her. You had to do it. I'll show you why.'

He produced a brief reconstruction of the story of Osiris and Isis. He had been the Osiris who had been shattered into a thousand fragments by the thunderbolt of the Medusa. She had been the Isis who had put the pieces together again. The details did not unfold. What unfolded fully was the picture of the reconstructed man, with the still, sad, fire-washed face of death. It was then that she was able to link up that particular expression with thousands and thousands of other people who had died terrible and violent deaths.

He sat so hard and so carefully on the long drama of human history, especially the darkness of horrors, that it was only when her life was assaulted like that that peeps into the boiling cauldron were allowed. She struggled over and over to link the brief snapshots, the statements he made and the torture of certain states of mind, into some coherent, broad, overall pattern. There was a strange parallel in her observations to mankind's myths – they began to seem vividly true. Nearly every nation had that background of mythology – looming, monstrous personalities they called 'the Gods', personalities who formed the base of their attitudes to royalty and class; personalities whose deeds were hideous and yet who assumed powerful positions, presumably because they were in possession of thunderbolts, like the Medusa. Then again the story was shaded down to a very personal level of how a man is overwhelmed by his own internal darkness; that when he finds himself in the embrace of Medusa she is really the direct and tangible form of his own evils, his power lusts, his greeds, his self-importance, and these dominate him totally and bring him to the death of the soul.

His only comment on the Osiris-Isis story was: 'It was the first work we did together and the first life you lived after your soul had been created. My death at that time broke the hold she had over me.'

It was two-handed, this work, a fight to liberate Sello from the death-grip of monstrous concubines alternating with a fight against Egyptian priesthood. No one knew what they did in those cloistered halls where they cultivated their powers and the powers of their Gods or royalty. But a shuddering mankind recorded the results: 'And she hath hissing serpents for her hair and her face turneth the beholder into stone . . .' The things of the soul had in reality been reduced to an Al Capone show of extreme cruelty. They were a people given to 'seeing' things and, through the purpose and structure of her soul, she gained easy access to the inner temples of dark secrets. But she was the new dream. Her chief role was that of blabbermouth, for when she stepped out into the sunlight she turned round and said: 'Well, folks, you want to know what we do in there? I'll show you. It's quite easy.' And how important their secret rituals were to them! They said: 'Who dunnit? Who spilled the beans?' And someone always said: 'Blabbermouth.'

Sello said to her at that time: 'They took you and threw you in a deep pit full of cockroaches and left you to die. So I took hold of one of them and threw him alive to the worms.'

Something had been churning over in his mind. This was his natural occupation, the things of the soul, the moral orders of mankind. The performance of Blabbermouth in the cloistered halls had given him the key to the future: 'Blabbermouth is right. Religion ought to be a function in which all mankind may participate. Ah, I'm gaining control of the God show again.'

It was like a liberation from many ailments, the abrupt rise from the ghastly deathbed of black-magic rituals, miracle-performing, cloistered halls, the insane, raving power-maniac world of the Pharaohs. As far as Elizabeth was concerned, he had a choice. He had seen the performance of the wife Isis. He preferred the performance of Blabbermouth in the Egyptian temples and made that the base of the long monastic friendship. The impressions of the friend who had walked towards Elizabeth were those of a man who had walked, moved, thought, lived and worked like a flame in the dark night. It was as though in the very beginning he had been handed the essential secrets, the essential clues to the evolution of the soul, but the theories this time were expounded against a new background; the wayside inn, the wayside well, shady trees and the courtyards of rich and poor friends. There was a new band of men, the monks, with bare feet and simple cloth draped around their forms, who addressed each other in loving terms and furrowed their brows in Socratic dialogues under the stars. It was so much for free that the wayside beggar could peer in with an enquiring face and join in the dialogues. The philosophies were spun around the everyday events of people's lives and included the animals, the flowers and the occupations of mankind. Then mankind said: 'We like it.' They remembered and kept records of philosophies so tentative and flexible that people could speculate on them endlessly, and add to them. They forgot the terrible monstrosities of the past they had called 'the Gods', who had hurled thunderbolts around with so little regard for the welfare of others, for anything except their own prestige, that civilization after civilization had disappeared in their holocausts. No longer did the concubines of a man like Sello rampage through towns hissing thunder and lightning out of their eyes and mouths. They were beautiful women who cried and wiped his feet with their long black hair. They seemed strangely soft and docile, but it had taken hell to break their power.

It was this period she was familiar with, the compassion and tenderness with which people regarded each other, the uncertainties of questing within, the lack of assertion and dominance. She could not comprehend the sudden introduction of Medusa, or the picture he showed her then of a Sello just before the time of the fall of man from godliness. She doubted he had ever been a God. He had looked then like a Caligula in little boots with thin stick legs. He had strutted around as the emperor of heaven. A woman he was after at the time – on the surface, a dazzling goddess – precipitated the first explosion. He was concentrating on her man, who did not have stick legs. She was concentrating on the prestige and power to be acquired from the position as God. They split two ways, wreaking havoc and wreckage on all sides. She was the first of the power-maniacs who knew their business, and knew what they could get out of being God. He was malicious. He had deeper insight. He could set traps and temptations they all tumbled into. There wasn't any kind of perversion and depravity they did not practice till today it lingers like a dark psychological stream of horrors in the courts of law. Then, at that time, it was a way of life, publicly, openly lived. He broke down and cried at last only because it was an open display of the powers of the soul. What she heard as he lifted the lid a bit was: 'I'm greater than you because my power is greater than yours. Yap, Yap, Yap. There, bam, you go, into oblivion, bastard!'

It was the quality of his soul-power which placed him at a disadvantage in these circumstances. She knew it because basically she was composed of the same material. It was, in its final state, passive, inactive, impersonal. It was linked in some way to the creative function, the dreamer of new dreams; and the essential ingredient in creativity is to create and let the dream fly away with a soft hand and heart. He was opposed by personalities whose powers, when activated, rumbled across the heavens like thunder. He had nothing its equivalent in this war. At some stage Medusa entered. She could hurl a thunderbolt like nothing ever seen before and shatter a victim into a thousand fragments: 'Who's running the show around here? I am. Who knows everything around here? I do. Who's wearing the pants in this house? I am.' She seemed to fill all requirements. Then he turned and showed Elizabeth a small, round, deep opening in the earth from which her soul had emerged. It was a black, shapeless mass with wings. Several companions accompanied her so that she would not be lonely, one of whom was eventually the Bathsheba whose soul he joined with that of Buddha's wife to pull him out of his withdrawn meditations on oblivion and eternity.

It seemed all right. He had a protector. And then it did not seem so right after a time. Some dark, evil thing set down roots deep into his soul and ate and ate and ate. It was smiling all the time while he moved from one depravity to another. It just kept on smiling and wriggling its broad hips. Depravity and perversion of the most base degree was its natural habitat. Did it matter then what a man slept with – a cow, a horse, a child or anything? A person who cries under conditions like that has retained enough sensitivity to look on his own degradation, and there is a point where he begins to fight his way to freedom. It took a shattering death to pull out the deep, dark roots. It took centuries of taut, religious discipline to give her a new kingdom and a peak of spirituality so intense, she was frightening to observe. The relationship had run its full course. He was saying a permanent goodbye. The clamour he set up was like a low, terrible moan throughout a whole year. He threw the burden of it on Elizabeth: 'You first liberated me from my demon. Now liberate me from my goddess.'

Elizabeth had never seen such a spineless, backboneless man. He was terrible about women when he had an obsession about them. At that time he was so frightened by the thunderbolt Medusa had hurled at Elizabeth that he quickly pulled out a photograph of the future. He was walking down the road, hand in hand, with a new girl, and his smile was quite something to see. How to get over the hurdle of the present into the happiness of the future? In the comedy and horror that unfolded, he seemed to be pushing forward all the nightmares of the past: 'If I don't let go of her she'll ruin the African continent the way we ruined so many civilizations together.' Elizabeth was given no opportunity to observe the magnificence of the real drama. Medusa was the true measure of his greatness as the prophet of mankind. He had taken sheer filth and muck and turned it into a glittering masterpiece of perfection.

Medusa was smiling. She had some top secret information to impart to Elizabeth. It was about her vagina. Without any bother for decencies she sprawled her long black legs in the air, and the most exquisite sensation travelled out of her towards Elizabeth. It enveloped Elizabeth from head to toe like a slow, deep, sensuous bomb. It was like falling into deep, warm waters, lazily raising one hand and resting in a heaven of bliss. Then she looked at Elizabeth and smiled, a mocking superior smile:

'You haven't got anything *near* that, have you?'

The mocking smile remained permanently attached to her face. It was maddening because it was even there when Elizabeth had her first mental breakdown, but it was not maddening to her to be told she hadn't a vagina. She might have had but it was not such a pleasant area of the body to concentrate on, possibly only now and then if necessary. But Medusa's next assault pulled the ground right from under Elizabeth's feet. She fell into a deep hole of such excruciating torture that, briefly, she went stark, raving mad.

Medusa said: 'Africa is troubled waters, you know. I'm a powerful swimmer in troubled waters. You'll only drown here. You're not linked up to the people. You don't know any African languages.'

She blamed Sello in the brown suit for it. They played on her experiences in South Africa. In South Africa she had been rigidly classified Coloured. There was no escape from it to the simple joy of being a human being with a personality. There wasn't any escape like that for anyone in South Africa. They were races, not people. She had lived for a time in a part of South Africa where nearly all the Coloured men were homosexuals and openly paraded down the street dressed in women's clothes. They tied turbans round their heads, wore lipstick, fluttered their eyes and hands and talked in high, falsetto voices. It was so widespread, so common to so many men in this town that they felt no shame at all. They and people in general accepted it as a disease one had to live with. No one commented at these strange men dressed in women's clothes. Sometimes people laughed when they were kissing each other in the street.

An African man gave her the most reasonable explanation: 'How can a man be a man when he is called boy? I can barely retain my own manhood. I was walking down the road the other day with my girl, and the Boer policeman said to me: "Hey, boy, where's your pass?" Am I a man to my girl or a boy? Another man addresses me as boy. How do you think I feel?'

Suddenly the nights became torture. As she closed her eyes all these Coloured men lay down on their backs, their penes in the air, and began to die slowly. Some of them who could not endure these slow deaths simply toppled over into rivers and drowned, Medusa's mocking smile towering over them all.

'You see, that's what you are like,' she said. 'That's your people, not African people. You're too funny for words. You have to die like them.'

There was a pressure turned on her, so powerful Elizabeth collapsed flat on her back. She just lay there nearly choked to death. It was like a wild, insistent chant in her ears: 'Die, die, die'. But a current was turned on, choking her. At the peak of it, when her mind was a riot of terror, the current was suddenly switched off. She saw the white-robed monk lean forward and set light to a stuffed effigy that resembled Medusa. A man's voice, unseen, said loudly in the room: 'I told him not to bring the doll to the altar.'

She fell into a deep, exhausted sleep, only to awaken the following morning to a greater terror still. Someone had turned on a record inside her head. It went on and on in the same, stuck groove: 'Dog, filth, the Africans will eat you to death. Dog, filth, the Africans will eat you to death.'

45

She washed and dressed, then had to comb her hair in the mirror. She flinched and looked away. There was an unnamable horror there. She could not endure to look at it. Her hands were shaking badly. How could someone run away from their own mind? The record was right inside her head: 'Dog, filth, the Africans will eat you to death. Dog, filth, the Africans will eat you to death.'

Dan later admitted that he had turned on the record. He and Sello were supposed to be friends who shared everything, including visions, and he claimed that he had gained an insight into everything at the same time as Sello. He had chosen the position of silent, unseen observer, but was suffering terribly because he was supposed to be frantically in love with her. He said something about their souls being 'joined together at the roots', so when Medusa put her in the torture-chamber he decided to add to it with the record. He could not endure the pain of his suppressed love. She ought to suffer too.

All Elizabeth could see was Medusa and the Sello in the brown suit. Apart from the first time, when he had snarled that he was God by himself, he left the management of everything to Medusa. She was enjoying herself. She kept one eye on Elizabeth and engaged in whispering consultations with brown-suit. They seemed to be saying: 'Ah, it's nearly time. She won't last long.'

The German woman she had lived with in South Africa had told her of how Jewish people awoke one morning to a nightmare like that. Prior to Hitler's propaganda they had just been like any other German citizens, with family lives and occupations. She came home one evening and remarked on an incident that had taken place in the office where she worked as a typist: 'I thought I was back in Hitler's Germany this morning,' she said. 'We have our tea served by a young African man. There's a small swing door at the entrance to our office, and he always comes in that way with the tea-tray. Well, this morning one of the Afrikaners in the office walked up to him and kicked the tray right out of his hands. The cups and sugar and milk all went flying around the place. The Afrikaner turned around to his fellows and burst out laughing. They joined in. I thought the man would be angry. Oh no, he cringed and laughed too. He said: "Ha, ha, baas." And I thought: "I've seen this somewhere. The Hitler Youth did this to the Jews. They were so demoralized by the propaganda, they cringed like this man. They began to believe they were inferior, but once the liberation came and the war was over it disappeared overnight. There was no sign of it in them." Then I thought, "The same will happen here. Once these people are free of the humiliation, there will not be a sign of it left." '

So many people ran away from South Africa to forget it or throw it off. It seemed impossible then, the recurring, monotonous song in her head: 'Dog, filth, the Africans will eat you to death. . . .' It broke her instantly. She could not help but identify with the weak, homosexual Coloured men who were dying before her eyes. One day of it set her nervous system screaming. A week of it reduced her to a total wreck. She lay on the bed trapped in misery. There was nothing she could think of, to counter it: 'I'm not like that. I've never been a racialist. Of course I admit I'm a Coloured. I'm not denying it. I'm not denying anything. Maybe people who are Coloureds are quite nice too, just like Africans. . . .'

Nothing turned off the record. She had not planned it. She had not been thinking along those lines at all, and the option of any sane, reasonable reply had been taken away from her. Was that why that kind of propaganda broke whole races of people? Someone just asserted something and directed it at a victim, regardless of whether it made sense or not: 'You are inferior. You are filth.' Their power of assertion was so tremendous the whole flow and interchange of life stopped before it. And yet, in her case, there had been a beautiful introduction to this unbelievable nightmare. Where was the white-robed monk who had captured and riveted her attention with his question-and-answer approach to life? Here was a world, now, where there were no questions, only pre-planned, overpowering statements that choked her, and an incredibly malicious man in a brown suit with a woman too shocking to comprehend. She could not say whether Medusa was human or animal. Medusa had human form and, regardless of anything she said or did, she remained her competent, confident, smiling self.

By Sunday evening, exhausted, she thought quietly to herself: 'Sello, after all, is just a fool, and he looks like a monkey.'

She closed her eyes, wearily. There was an instant attack from Medusa. She stood next to brown-suit and said, accusingly: 'You see, she says you look like a monkey. What are you going to do about it?'

As Elizabeth watched, brown-suit's face slowly changed to the shape of an owl. He said: 'Oh no, I'm not a monkey. I'm a wise old owl.'

She jerked upright in bed. What was this? Did it mean she had no privacy left? She had only been thinking, not saying anything out loud. So broken was she that she immediately fell into a defensive argument, muttering out loud to herself. 'Of course it's true. He looks like a monkey. He's so ugly. I'm not saying I'm not ugly myself. I shouldn't mind if anyone told me I'm ugly because I know it's true. Does it mean, if God looks ugly one ought not to say so without being dreadfully punished for saying so? Agh, I don't really care if I look like the backside of a donkey....'

A hissing, insistent undertone accompanied her thoughts: 'Yes, you think like that because you hate Africans. You don't like the African hair. You don't like the African nose....'

She turned her head this way and that, struggling for an escape from the torment. A faint glow of light appeared in the small window of her mud hut. It was dawn. She sprang eagerly out of bed. It was an excuse to fetch some water and make tea or do anything, except suffocate. She picked up the empty water-bucket, walked to the door, opened it, then stood transfixed to the spot, her eyes wide with horror. An owl lay stone dead on the doorstep.

She backed into the room and closed the door. There was a confused roar in her head. She immediately linked the owl's death to the events of the night, and began muttering incoherently to herself again. There was an overpowering sense of evil, and she wasn't sure if she had or had not killed the owl. But a longing for a cup of tea pushed through her terrified mutterings.

'I think that owl must have suddenly died of old age,' she

thought, reasoning with herself. 'A branch of the tree outside hangs right over my hut. It must have been sitting on that branch when it died.'

She picked up the water-bucket, opened the door, took a flying leap over the dead owl. It was winter and cold outside. She was shaking from head to foot, so badly that the water-bucket kept bumping against her leg and spilling its contents on to her nightdress. Nor did her teeth stop chattering until she had taken the first sip of tea. People only function well when their inner lives are secure and peaceful. She was like a person driven out of her own house while demons rampaged within, turning everything upside down. It was the beginning of the school holidays. She had no work to do, except go into the central part of Motabeng village and make a few purchases. The small boy awoke quietly. He clutched in one hand a toy car, took in the other a bowl of porridge and sat down on the mat. Then he totally disregarded the porridge and concentrated all his attention on circling the car round the bowl.

'Eat your porridge,' she said, helplessly.

He looked up at her with a pair of unconcerned black eyes. He went on circling the car.

'I'm not going to take you shopping,' she said.

'I'll follow you,' he said, firmly.

She stood up and started to dress. He let out a loud wail: 'Why don't you dress me first? You want to go away and leave me.'

Her head was throbbing with pain from a sleepless and feverish night. She grabbed a pile of his clothes off a chair and said irritably: 'You'd like to be slaughtered, hey? Shut your mouth, you damn little nuisance.'

He took all his moods from her and imitated her in every way. A day which started off like this could throw him off balance completely. Suddenly, he seemed to sense something funny in the air and mimicked in a shrill voice: 'You'd like to be slaughtered, hey? Shut your mouth, you damn little nuisance.'

'Put your car down,' she said. 'You can't dress holding a car in your hand.'

A wicked gleam shot into his eyes. He clutched the car

in a vice-grip: 'Put your car down,' he mimicked. 'You can't dress holding a car in your hand.'

'You're at death's door, my son,' she said, murderously.

'You're at death's door, my son,' he shrilled.

She sat down on the bed and burst into tears. He stood looking at her for a moment, his eyes turned big and solemn. Something's really wrong here, they seemed to say. How often had something not been wrong over the past months? There were only stormy seas in his house, and he was frequently tossed this way and that in the storm. His mother's concentration was riveted elsewhere. He straightened himself with a quaint, manly air:

'I can show you I know how to dress myself,' he said, haughtily. 'I can put my own shoes on. I can eat my porridge.'

He sat down on the floor again and grimly concentrated on eating his porridge. People who had mothers like he had were lost if they did not know how to care for themselves. She looked at him in a sort of agony and thought: 'Journeys into the soul are not for women with children, not all that dark heaving turmoil. They are for men, and the toughest of them took off into the solitude of the forests and fought out their battles with hell in deep seclusion. No wonder they hid from view. The inner life is ugly.'

She was breaking under the strain of it. She walked into the central part of the village holding the small boy by the hand, and the ugliness of the inner torment was abruptly ripped open and exposed to public view. She turned into a shop and stood abstractedly at a counter, not having any idea of what she wanted to buy. In front of her were some transistor radios. The shop assistant said: 'Can I help you, madam?'

She said it three times before Elizabeth looked up at her and nodded dumbly. She blindly picked up a small radio and handed it to the girl for wrapping up. The girl said: 'You must first go into that office over there and record the purchase. The clerk has to inform the post office of every radio we sell, as you have to pay for the radio licence.'

She entered the office. From that moment her eyes remained riveted to his face and she began pitching and heaving mentally in a crescendo of torture. The insistent hiss, hiss of horror swamped her mind: 'You see,' it said. 'You don't really like Africans. You see his face? It's vacant and stupid. He's slow-moving. It takes him ages to figure out the brand name of the radio. You never really liked Africans. You only pretended to. You have no place here. Why don't you go away....'

She was choking for air. The clerk had told her to sit down opposite him. A loud wail of counter-protest was arising in her. The insistent hissing was mean, stifling, vicious. Whom could she accuse, to end it? She sprang to her feet, slamming the chair back against the wall, and shouted: 'Oh, you bloody bastard Batswana!! Oh, you bloody bastard Batswana!!' Then she simply opened her mouth in one long, high piercing scream.

People came running from all directions and were blocked in a crowd at the entry to the office. Someone broke through the crowd, a heavily built man with a beard. His face was screwed up with anxiety. He was talking and shaking her by the arm. She could not hear. An ice-cold sweat bathed her from head to toe, and everything became dimmer and dimmer until she couldn't see at all.

It was such an impossible situation for the small boy, he just ignored it completely and went on circling his car on the floor where he was seated. People looked at him and shook their heads sadly. The man with the beard was holding on to the swaying form. He said to the clerk: 'Ring up for the ambulance. Let's get her to hospital. She's very ill.'

She opened her eyes in a bed of the private ward of the Motabeng hospital. A doctor stood near by. He bent down and said gently: 'What's wrong with you?'

She turned her face away and said, with extreme misery: 'I don't like people.'

'It's all right,' he said. 'You can stay here until you feel better.'

She tried to raise her leaden head from the pillow: 'What happened to my son? Where is he?'

'He's just outside the door. He's with the principal of the Motabeng Secondary School, who brought you to hospital.

The principal would like to talk to you. Shall I tell him to come in?'

The heavily-built bearded man walked in, holding the small boy by the hand. He blinked his greenish-brown eyes uncertainly and sat down on the chair beside the bed. He put the boy on his knee. The boy was still tightly clutching his toy car. She had seen the man often in the central part of Motabeng village, but apart from a distant greeting had never had occasion to talk to him. He was extremely reserved, aloof and morose by temperament, and often walked around with• the gloom of doomsday on his face. He was an Afrikaner man from South Africa and the founder of the Motabeng Secondary School. He said, simply: 'My wife will take care of your son until you come out of hospital. We are both refugees and must help each other.'

She was too stunned mentally to say anything beyond a 'Thank you.'

He furrowed his brow and offered some personal inform- ation: 'I suffer, too, because I haven't a country and know what it's like. A lot of refugees have nervous breakdowns.'

She tried to raise her leaden head: 'I want to tell you something,' she said. 'There's something torturing me. There are strange under-currents and events here. . . .'

He averted his face quickly. He did not want to hear any details about the country or anything else, simply accepting the fact that she had had a nervous breakdown out of the blue. He stood up and set the boy on the ground. The child turned round once and threw her a quiet look of sympathy, as much as to say: 'I knew there was something wrong with you this morning.' He raised one hand slightly in a secretive good-bye gesture and walked out with the man. A nurse walked in with a tray and set it down on a table near the bed. She smiled in a pretty, kind way and said:

'Turn over, I'm going to give you a shot to put you to sleep.'

The world seemed strangely peaceful. The storm in her head had subsided. It had taken such drastic clamour to silence the hissing record in her head, but it had left a terrible wound. She could feel it bleeding and bleeding and bleeding, quietly. Her so-called analytical mind was being shattered to pieces. It depended on questions and more questions, tentative propositions, with all the time and patience in eternity to solve the riddles, and the joy of friendly and affectionate exchanges. A darkness of immense dimensions had fallen upon her life. She could only hear the yapping of potential exterminators. She turned over and pressed her head into the pillow. People cried out so often in agony against racial hatreds and oppressions of all kinds. All their tears seemed to be piling up on her, and the source or roots from which they had sprung were being exposed with a vehement violence. For she thought that the nurse had left the room some time ago, yet there was a white form standing beside her bed. She raised her head a little. It was Sello. There was a still, remote look in his face. He said: 'I have to show you some things. Come.'

She found herself faced with a deep cesspit. It was filled almost to the brim with excreta. It was alive, and its contents rumbled. Huge angry flies buzzed over its surface with a loud humming. He caught hold of her roughly behind the neck and pushed her face near the stench. It was so high, so powerful, that her neck nearly snapped off her head at the encounter. She whimpered in fright. She heard him say, fiercely: 'She made it. I'm cleaning it up. Come, I'll show you what you made.'

He suddenly turned into an enormous sky-bird with powerful, soaring wings. Was there ever a man whose heights and depths were so extreme they were totally disassociated from each other, as though they faced each other with blank eyes, neither recognizing the other for centuries and centuries? For he had talked, ever since she could recall, only of this pale blue heaven that had shaped itself around the souls of men. And out of it had thundered the great dramas of nobility and sacrifice that became the blueprints of perfection for many nations. It was a belonging-to-no-one-in-particular world, where kings had earned crowns and never worn them for crowns, and oppression and slavery were the same name. And they said men overcame their passions there and rose to the majestic stature of gods with flashing eyes and wild, freedom-loving souls. And they created and dreamt and sang only in the byways of life, as though there had been a mutual agreement all round to shun sham and pomp and applause as the things which led to the death of the soul. And love was like a girl walking down a road on staggering legs with the wind blowing through her hair. And love was like a girl with wonder in her eyes. And love was like a girl with a flaming heart and impulsive arms. And love was so many things, so many variations on one theme: humility and equality – for when those men said: 'Is it possible? Could you love me?', thrones and kingdoms were of no account against the power of love.

They pray, so falsely: from the heart of God let love enter the hearts of men, thus removing the things of the soul to some impossibly unseen, mystical heaven. Oh no, a heaven had been planned directly around the hearts of men and as, bit by bit, its plan unfolded they called it so many names: democracy, freedom of thought, social consciousness, protest, human rights, exploration, moral orders, principles and a thousand and one additions for the continual expansion and evolution of the human soul.

'An intelligence is behind it all,' people said. It was mankind's universal knowing of the fall and the dark times when civilizations were swallowed up in holocausts; when powers of increasing evil fought to the death over the small bones of their own self-importance and lusts and greed.

And out of the shifting patterns of tenderness and co-operation before her gaze she formulated her own broad definition of God: God is the totality of all great souls and their achievements; the achievements are not that of one single, individual soul, but of many souls who all worked to make up the soul of God, and this might be called God, or the Gods. She floated slowly back to everyday reality on this huge tidal wave of peace.

Someone was touching her arm. It was the night-duty nurse.

'I've brought you some tea,' she said, smiling. 'You must be hungry. You've been sleeping for fifteen hours.'

Elizabeth sat up abruptly, flung off the bedclothes and swung her legs off the bed. Her head was clear and sparkling. The nurse started back in surprise: 'Yo!' she said in Setswana. 'And where do you think you're going now?' She pointed to a card at the top of the bed: Patient very ill. Do not disturb.

'I'm quite better,' Elizabeth said. 'I want to go home.'

The nurse shook her head: 'You like to frighten people,' she said. 'Day-duty nurse recorded total collapse. She told me she did not think you would be alive in the morning. You can't jump about like that. You must go back to bed.'

Elizabeth looked at the nurse and laughed. She had been thrown a powerful life-line, as though by turning inwards she had found that the centre of herself was still sane and secure, and that the evils which had begun to dominate her mind had a soaring parallel of goodness. It seemed to be all that mattered, a reassurance of a goodness that was like a still, steady, deathless flame. She argued vehemently. There was no one to take care of her son. She couldn't just lie here and depend on other people while she was feeling quite well, in every way. By ten o'clock she was swinging her way out of the hospital gates. The still, blue sky of winter, with its soft shimmering haze, corresponded to the hazy warmth and peace in her own heart. She stood on a dusty road, waiting for a taxi to take her the five miles out of the village to Motabeng Secondary School.

The bush began just at the edge of Motabeng and contrasted vividly in beauty with the starkness of central village with its endless circles of mud huts. The bush was a wild, expansive landscape dotted with wind-bent, umbrella-shaped thorn trees. It stretched for miles and miles in all directions, and far off in the distance low blue hills lay like slumbering giants in an eternal sleep. Motabeng Secondary School had been built right amidst this wilderness of solitude and slumber. The taxi stopped outside the school gates. She half turned to enter, then turned again and looked down a long brown road that wound and wound its way off into the distance, linking Motabeng to a village thirty-six miles away. She had not had enough of her own peace and longed to hold on to it for as long as possible.

She started walking down the dusty brown road. The school fence continued for about half a mile. On the other side of the road a small settlement of mud huts had sprung up overnight. Some of the village women had found employment at the school as housekeepers and nursemaids for the children of the teaching staff. She stopped at the end of the school fence and looked up. . . . A bird sang in a tree nearby; a long, deep, trilling melody, heightened to an intense sweetness by the silence. A grey-brown wild rabbit scampered with long, alarmed, flapping ears across the road and some insects in the rough, brown, wind-torn grass communed in plaintive, brooding soliloquies with their own selves.

'One day, I'm going to live here,' she thought, never dreaming that three months later this was to be the situation of her first home.

SHe turned, climbed over the fence and walked through the school grounds to the principal's home. It was built on a slight rise overlooking the school buildings. He used his home as an office during the day and his wife, a quiet pretty woman, sat at a nearby table typing out his enormous correspondence and endless pamphlets on educational programmes for developing countries. He looked up astonished at her entry: 'I thought you'd be in hospital for some time,' he said. 'Your son isn't here. He's out playing in the fields or somewhere with our son. They'll be home about twelve and you can wait here if you like.'

'I'll make some tea, Eugene,' his wife said, rising.

The bearded man, Eugene, turned back to his writing. He sat in a chair near the window. Only as he sipped his tea did he turn around and speak to her briefly.

'You don't seem to get along with the local people,' he observed.

'It's not that,' Elizabeth said, anxiously. 'People don't care here whether foreigners get along with them or not. They are deeply absorbed in each other.' She paused and laughed. 'They have a saying that Batswana witchcraft only works on a Motswana, not an outsider. I like the general atmosphere because I don't care whether people like me or not. I am used to isolation.'

'Too much isolation isn't a good thing for anyone,' he said.

He put down his cup and returned to his writing. She looked out of the window at the sprawling arrangement of low, whitewashed buildings. It was a vast empire, built on almost nothing but voluntary labour of all kinds. They had dug out the thorn bushes and wild scrub-grass and replaced them with fruit trees, vegetable gardens, chicken houses and, in the distance, gently swaying fields of corn. It was a school where inventions and improvisations of all sorts appeared because someone from another land always had a new solution to offer to any problem which arose. Words like skill, work, fullest development of personality and intellect recurred again and again in the pamphlets the man Eugene wrote, but in those fluid, swiftly-written papers circulated among all teachers they quivered on the pages with a life all their own. They conjured up in the minds of the poor and starving a day when every table would overflow with good food; roast chicken, roast potatoes, boiled carrots, rice and puddings. They felt in every way like food and clothes and opportunities for everyone. It wasn't like that in his country, South Africa. There they said the black man was naturally dull, stupid, inferior, but they made sure to deprive him of the type of education which developed personality, intellect, skill. So many deeper insights had been unfolding before her which provided clues as to what moved men like Eugene to oppose death and evil and greed, and surround themselves with a creative ferment. It was out of death itself that a great light had been found. Sello had said: 'Everything was wrong until I broke down and cried. . . .' Had this man, too, looked on a deep evil of racial hatred and broken down and cried? Something was going drastically wrong with her own life. Just the other day she had broken down and cried. Her loud wail had only the logic of her inner torment, but it was the same thing; the evils overwhelming her were beginning to sound like South Africa from which she had fled. The reasoning, the viciousness were the same, but this time the faces were black and it was not local people. It was large, looming soul personalities.

She couldn't even begin to say: 'Well, you know Sello, don't you? He isn't all he seems to be on the surface – the progressive Botswana farmer, eager to discuss the latest agricultural techniques. He's really Dr Jekyll and Mr Hyde. And he confided some extraordinary things to me, so I'm not sure I'm quite normal any more. I don't think people who conduct telepathic relationships with other people are normal anyway, but I never thought it would happen to me. I could swear I've been dead sane all along, for all my life, till now. In fact, I'm astonished to see the blue sky today. And you know what sort of world I live in? It's midnight all the time. I'd not taken note of it. I'd not taken note of real living people because so many fantastic images surround me, and they talk and move all the time, and when they address me I just burst out with the right lines on cue as though I am living with a strange "other self" I don't know so well. And you know Sello? He has a terrible Medusa hidden away in his subconscious. She's so real to me that I live in terror of her all my days. That's why I broke down. It's Medusa. She scared me from the first moment I saw her. She's unlike any other woman I've ever seen in my life before. She's haughty, arrogant, and there's some awful things unfolding here. . . . I feel frightened and lost. . . .'

She started a little. She had said her last thoughts out loud. The man looked up quietly and said in a simple way:

'I'll help you.'

It was the only way he revealed his passionate identity with his own country. He had said that to many South African refugees.

She had to choke back a rush of words. When had she not faced all the sorrows of life alone? There had never been anyone near when she had stood alone on street corners in South Africa and stared forlornly at a life without love. There wasn't anyone near her in the solitary, unfolding mental drama of torture in Motabeng village. The man's instinctive sympathy and offer of help was the nearest any human being had approached her isolation, and she could see that he was working on the simple theory that South Africans usually suffered from some form of mental aberration, so she only nodded her head in agreement to his offer of assistance.

The two small boys came panting and laughing up the stairs. Her son walked straight over to her and bumped himself against her knee. He looked up with sparkling black eyes – the butterflies he had chased after, the caterpillars he had caught and squashed, the wild race across the scrub-grass were clearly visible pictures in his eyes. He burst out, impulsively: 'Jimmy is my best friend.' The truth was he usually said that about anyone who palled up with him, once even about an old Motswana man of sixty who had sat down on the floor with him and chatted with him about the mystery of the animal life in the bush. She heard the other small boy set up a loud argument with his mother in the kitchen. He was very domineering. He moaned: 'You haven't any lunch for me, and I'm so hungry.'

'Lunch will be ready in a few minutes, Jimmy,' his mother said.

'Well, hurry up about it,' Jimmy said, offhandedly.

'Don't you talk to me like that, Jimmy!' his mother said, crossly.

The small boy Jimmy wandered out of the kitchen in a huff. Elizabeth could see that this little Jimmy, like her own son, was an imitator of some other adult in that household. He walked with the rolling gait of a stocky seaman, scratched his head absent-mindedly, blinked his eyes uncertainly and flopped down in a chair with his legs sprawled out like a grown man. He looked at Elizabeth and observed in a quaint, old-man voice: 'I heard you were ill?'

'Yes,' she said.

'I'm very sorry to hear that,' he said, nodding his head, wisely.

In the corner, from his work desk, his father let out one abrupt snort of laughter.

It was sunset when she arrived back at her hut in the central part of Motabeng. Someone had removed the dead owl from the doorstep, otherwise the area in which she lived was deserted at this time of the year. The women of the village were away at their lands, gathering in the summer harvest of corn. They would be back towards the end of the month, and she knew that one of her friends, Thoko, who usually supplied her with tit-bits of village gossip, would bring over a gift of watermelon and pumpkin. Elizabeth had lived for over two rainy seasons in Motabeng and the beginning of the rainy season always seemed a magical time to her. Women gathered up their possessions in a big bundle of cloth, heaved it on top of their heads, slung a hoe over their shoulders and set out with long, firm, determined strides to their lands.

'We are going to plough,' they said.

She could only stare after them, wistfully. It was not a part of her life; so many aspects of village life escaped her. And yet, it was one thing to walk into a greengrocer's shop in a town and pick up neatly-wrapped parcels of potatoes, tomatoes and onions; it was another to hold Thoko's pumpkin, which she had produced with her own hands. Who ever cared about farmers in a town? Why, if vegetables came out of a machine, it was one and the same thing to a town dweller. They were just there, ready made. But here, it was Thoko and the ploughing season and one and a half dozen high dramas in a bush life, shrouded in mystery. She had once asked Thoko if she could accompany her to her lands during the school holidays, to plough, and Thoko had looked at her with wide, shocked eyes.

'A foreigner like you would die in one day, it's so dangerous,' she had protested. 'Do you know what happened to me when I was pulling the plough? A great big Mamba snake jumped out of the ground and ran over my body; tsweeee, like lightning! I dropped dead on the ground with shock. The cattle jumped high in the air! In the night the jackals come and cry around the hut. They want the meat which we hang up in the trees. Then there is a great wild cat, like a leopard. We are afraid to rest and fall asleep under the trees. He comes around softly and with one smash of his paw cracks open our skulls and eats our brains. He always puts the skin back nicely over the eaten part and when we find people dead like that, we know the wild cat is about. . . .'

These gruesome details of life in the bush made Elizabeth shudder from end to end. She cancelled totally the idea of being that kind of farmer who earned her year's supply of food in breakneck battles with dangerous wild animals. But a great wonder about the soil and the food it produced had been aroused. The slowly drifting closeness to the soil was increased by living in a mud hut. It was like living with the trees and insects right indoors, because there was no sharp distinction between the circling mud walls of a hut and the earth outside. And the roof always smelt of mouldy grass, and all kinds of insects made their homes in the grass roof and calmly deposited their droppings on the bed, chair, table and floor.

So she spent most of the holidays of the rainy season taking long walks across Motabeng village with the small boy, absorbed by the sky which had turned itself into a huge back-drop for the swaying, swirling movements of the desert rain. Sometimes the rain fell in soft, glistening streams over the village, shot through with sunlight, and all the roofs of the mud huts changed to pure gold. Sometimes the horizon rain came sweeping over Motabeng in one enormous white-packed cumulus cloud driven by high wind and suddenly emptied itself in one violent, terrific and deafening roar over the village. It seemed to heighten and deepen the rambling labyrinth of her inner life, which, like the sky of Motabeng in the summer time, swayed and swirled with subterranean upheavals. In moments of vast, expansive peace like that evening, she liked to imagine that she was gathering all the threads of life together and holding them in her hands. There was an added touch of sound, solid sanity through that one, almost day-long contact with the family life of the man, Eugene. She put the small boy to sleep on his mattress on the floor and sat on the bed, broodingly sipping a cup of tea, reflecting, shut in briefly, on her own self. There was a half-eager stirring in her. The practical genius of the Eugene man excited her interest. It was so broad and impersonal, so free and unconcerned and such a sharp contrast to the nightmares which had propelled her own breakdown that she ran and re-ran the events of the day over and over in her mind, with a simple, child-like joy.

But seemingly happiness of any kind was not her immediate programme. The hard conflict of good and evil in arid terrain crashed down into her consciousness as soon as she closed her eyes in the dark. There was Medusa. She was smiling, mockingly. She held a plate of food in her hands and, offering it to Elizabeth, said: 'Are you sick? Eat this food.'

Elizabeth accepted the plate. As she raised a spoonful of the food to her mouth, Medusa snatched away the plate and yapped:

'Don't eat too much. You're too fat.'

61

Her second-in-command, Sello in the brown suit, nodded his head. There was a mean expression in his eyes. Detached from it all sat Sello the monk. It was against him that she was to slowly develop a deep, black rage. He was clearly using her as a focus for his observations of Medusa and Sello of the brown suit. He sat there staring at them fixedly, unmovingly, without any censure. There was no one to censure Medusa the way the poor of Africa had walked in and censured both Sello and Elizabeth. Yet she claimed those people as her people. Why were they not there to sort out the moral logic of her deeds, to offer comments on questions of good or evil? Medusa was simply given a wide, free field to display her major preoccupations, the main priority of which was the elimination of Elizabeth. She had a lot more thunderbolts in reserve, none as painful and deadly as her first blast, but each time they hit her Elizabeth would topple over, collapse and remain in bed for two days on end. Even if she wanted to, she could not retaliate in any way. She had no flashes of lightning, bolts, powers of the spirit or anything like that. There was just this loosely-knit, shuffling ambiguous mass which was her personality. Was that why she was so easy to kill on almost any occasion? She followed Sello's reasoning up to a certain point, but later came to the conclusion that, like Medusa, he too wanted to eliminate her. Of one thing she was sure, his initial presentation of constructive goodness in images and pictures had been a put-together whole of observations and tentative feelers he had put out towards the souls of others. He had presented it to Elizabeth as a form of teaching, deliberately manipulating the words and gestures of the people who had approached her. As soon as Medusa entered the picture, he became oblivious to everything but the arguments he conducted with his own tortured heart. His line of reasoning went something like this:

'Oh, she's meant everything to me. The future is unthinkable without her, and yet the relationship has run its full course and this is the end of it. There might be a loop-hole somewhere, something I can latch on to, to make the relationship evolve into something new and so perpetuate it. There's something disturbing me; a part of my present evolution is African, and I hear the beginnings of a great symphony, a complete statement for the future about the dignity of man, where none is high and none is low but all are equal. The difficulty here is that it hasn't yet swelled up to a loud and conscious declaration of the African future. We are a rising civilization. The surface of life here is narrow, stifling and full of petty prejudice. It is a world with the power to turn in on itself and keep its own secrets. That was the kind of world we operated in in the dark times, so narrow, so exclusive, so shut in that scavengers arose and ate whatever was in sight, leaving nothing over for the ordinary man. Did I care a damn? I was top-class royalty in those days and so was she. Let the ordinary man be my teacher this time and see what he has to say. Ah, you see, it's more terrible in Africa than anywhere else. They don't give a damn for my status as spiritual superman. There's no such thing as the superman here, that is, if I'm living as a man I'm human and fallible like everyone else. People who have been despised for so long know evil at its roots. Let me work out my ties to her along human and fallible lines. As for my mystical madonna, I dare not even look at her or else I am lost. Let me take a portion of the darkness and a portion of the light and combine it into the form of a woman I might still love. . . .'

And throughout that whole year Medusa only replied in despicable terms, the wrong things were stressed. When someone says 'my people' with a specific stress on the blackness of those people, they are after kingdoms and permanently child-like slaves. 'The people' are never going to rise above the status of 'the people'. They are going to be told what is good for them by the 'mother' and the 'father'. And she made the wrong kinds of attacks on Elizabeth. Too many people the world over were becoming mixed breeds and shading themselves down to browns and yellows and creams. And then, she could have chosen any other woman but Elizabeth to declaim her sexual superiority to. Sex had never counted in the strenuous turmoil of destiny behind Elizabeth, but long years of prison confinements had, death had, loss, suffering and sacrifice had, or else what did love really mean?

Sello, the monk, had proclaimed this very road in opposition to horrors – let people be free to evolve, let everything alone and re-create a new world of soft textures and undertones, full of wild flowers and birds and children's playtime and women baking bread. He kept on looking hopefully at Medusa. Oh no, she simply wanted to be the manager of the African continent with everyone she found disagreeable – OUT. He fell back on a haggard pose, shrinking and shrinking in size until his monk's cloth began to flap on his person like a scarecrow's rags. From the Sello in the brown suit issued a low moan of anguish. He seemed to be desperately attached to that thing Medusa had which no other woman had. And even this was a mockery. It was abnormally constructed, like seven thousand vaginas in one, turned on and operating at white heat. And an atmosphere of brutal desire pervaded everything, stagnated everything, and the wrenching, miserable battle of fierce tug-of-war stretched on and on with no end in sight. The contents of the cesspit leapt high into the air like an erupting volcano.

'I can't think along these lines,' Elizabeth moaned, over and over. If someone had promised to help someone there had been no warning of a journey right through hell. The radius of hell seemed endless. There were dancing-girls on the road in blue silk pants with the confused roar of Sodom and Gomorrah and Moloch behind them, there were perverts of all kinds who had jumped on the bandwagon of wilful evil with glee, and one weird little girl who rolled her eyes with mock innocence and said: 'I like to sleep with my daddy.' When Elizabeth picked her up she turned round and bit her on the hand. She didn't like the party spoilt in any way. And the way they smiled! That was all Elizabeth could not do; otherwise she was immersed in the filth from head to toe. It was like swallowing it whole, and the ordinary pleasures of life, like eating food, became an excruciating misery. It was as if excreta were everywhere. A panic to conceal the horror of her observations further confused her thought-processes. She strained uphill against the downward pull, but the effort to create counter-themes of goodness to the evil was so immense, it was like the feeble flayings in the air of a beetle flung helplessly on its back. Here was a world of no appeal. Here one could cry and cry and cry without any answer to suffering, Medusa providing the only contrast in this inhuman world. Nothing affected her adversely. She moved powerfully, busily, fearlessly under circumstances which made Elizabeth sick to the point of death. She had really earned the title of protector of Caligula, the strutting emperor of heaven in the time when evil had been totally assertive and conscience non-existent. To submit to evil and learn from it was not as easy as those seemingly straightforward truthful statements Sello had made in the beginning. Evil is a complexity so monumental that everything becomes a tangle of lies.

Where did the great gap of blank, shut-eye goodness fit in? For that's what monks were, delicately-buffered pillars of principles and platitudes. They sat under Bodhi trees and reviewed all their past lives. They said they had conversations with the forces of evil but this did not scare them. Some counter-majesty of the soul made the evil one cower and shudder. Then after forty days of disciplined meditation, they arose and gathered around them men of like mind and majestic soul-stature. They said:

'Brother, I have seen certain things in hell (never explicitly defined). These things urge me to advise you to overcome passion, pride, grasping and greed. I have overcome passion myself and am in full control of my senses. . . .'

They were men with a fantastic ability to take as wives madonnas who met them half way in their pursuit of God. If she accepted as true the small chunks of the past thrown at her by Sello, then the meditations under the Bodhi tree were as precarious and uncertain as any venture in life. God was no security for the soul. She accepted Sello's half-concealed revelation of the descent from Buddha to David of the Jews and balanced it against what was recorded of that tumultuous, turbulent life – the innate nobility, the deep God-contact, the peculiar Al Capone-like murder of Uriah and the explosive exposure, an exposure as ruthless and vehement as the murder; the long and tortuous suffering as atonement for the murder; the continuous interjections and advice of the prophets: 'God said it had to be this way. Now God said murder is actually a grievous crime. It creates a long cycle of retribution. Well, David, eat up all your retribution in one life through calamity after calamity. . . .'

The confusion of the prophet's interjections, the orders from God, the dubiousness of the woman involved, the passionate attachment to the woman all took on the strange logic of deliberate planning. So harsh was the present face-to-face view of evil that in a subconscious way Elizabeth found her mind turning with relief to African realism: a woman was simply a woman with legs; a man simply a man with legs, and if good and noble they earned a certain courteous respect, just as Christianity and God were courteous formalities people had learned to enjoy with mental and emotional detachment – the real battlefront was living people, their personalities, their treatment of each other. A real, living battle of jealousy, hate and greed was more easily understood and resolved under pressure than soaring, mystical flights of the soul.

Her exterior life had a painful way of coinciding with her inner torment. Three weeks later, as she entered the school grounds, she lost her job. The principal, a tall, thin Motswana man, handed her a letter from the school board. He was grinning. He knew its contents: 'We have received a report that you have been shouting and swearing at people in public. Such behaviour is unbecoming to a teacher. We are doubtful of your sanity, and request that you submit to us a certificate of sanity from a medical officer within fourteen days of receipt of this notice.'

She put the letter in her bag and turned to walk away. The principal rushed after her and grabbed her arm. He was still grinning but discomforted, flustered.

'Where are you going?' he demanded.

'I'm not working here any more,' she said, quietly.

'You can't do that,' he said. 'You can't just walk out. It's no trouble to get the certificate. Why don't you go and see the doctor?'

He would not let go of her arm. There was a confusion of hatred and anxiety on his face. On the one hand, someone like her, who went around saying 'bloody bastard Batswana', deserved to lose her job. On the other, there was an appalling sense of scandal in the air. They could not pin-point it.

They did not know what it was, except that she frightened them deeply. A group of teachers descended on them. He became quite hysterical, defending himself to them in Setswana. She tried to pull her arm free, near to tears. She wouldn't have made it anyway as a teacher for long. The inner storm was too high, too terrible.

A male teacher who stood a little apart spoke up in a voice of quiet command: 'Leave her. Let her go.'

There was a murmur of general agreement. They really disliked her and preferred to have nothing to do with her. There had been whispered secrets among themselves, a few alarmèd open remarks followed by a bewildering silence.

She walked a little way down the pathway from the school. The school bell rang. She stopped. Her class would have no teacher. The children were a teacher's heaven. Education was so hard to come by. They concentrated over-intensely, over-eagerly on their lessons. They paid for an education in schools so ill-equipped the teachers had no reference books and had to rake up information from their own brains on the structure of the skin and the tropical rain-forests of Africa. English composition was the starkest, bleakest lesson of the day. Someone had set the pattern, and it remained the furthest reach of the children's imaginations: Life In Botswana – 'When the rain rains we go to the lands to plough. We plough with oxen. The cow is a very useful animal. We use every part of it. We sell its skin for leather. We sell its bones. Glue is made from its hooves. . . .' They trusted nothing else. It was safe and thoroughly known by heart. Topics like Play-time In Motabeng, My Mother and Father, The Weather, Sunrise and Sunset, Birds Of Botswana started off with a few straggling sentences in incomprehensible English and strayed desperately into: 'When the rain rains . . .' It was totally impossible also to change the formula to: 'When it rains . . .' Children are great imitators, but the radius of imitation had already, by the time she received her class, been severely restricted to barren ground. There was a small bear of her childhood memories named Fuzzy Wuzzy. He went for a holiday by the seaside and ate an enormous pink and white ice-cream. She had not rested until she had lived out, to the last detail, all his holiday adventures. Children's literature and writing was often the most magical world, and yet there were harsh environments like this where all magic was dead or had not even begun to live. Everything was touched by this harshness. They ate no breakfast in the early morning, and by midday their mouths were white and pinched with starvation. Other children had soft mounds of butter where their cheeks ought to be, and dimpled smiles. The children she had taught were stark, gaunt, thin, like the twisted thorn-bush. So, if she cried about one thing, she cried about other things too. Pain was not only pain. It was a blinding daze of agony piling up on all sides. The only sane centre of purposeful, expanding and hopeful activity in this desolation was the Motabeng Secondary School. She walked home, dismissed a young girl who was caring for her son and with him took a taxi once again to the home of the Eugene man. Hadn't he said: 'I'll help you'?

He did. He read the letter from the school board without comment, then turned round and asked: 'Do you have any plans?' She had none. He had a thousand and one things going on at the same time. There was the secondary school catering for GCE students. Once that had been securely established, he had spread out the network of his educational programme to include elementary-school leavers with no future. They formed the youth-development work-groups of the school and acquired skills in building, carpentry, electricity, printing, shoe-making, farming and textile work. Once this had been securely established, he turned his attention to the poor, illiterate villager. In him were the beginnings of local industry. His house was already a clutter of hand-made goods; mats, blankets, baskets, wooden bowls and spoons, handbags of rough woven string and, in one corner of the room, a huge elementary loom for hand-made woven blankets. He walked to a cupboard and took out a collection of odd-looking objects, among which were a piece of roughly made candle, a bar of crude washing-soap and a smaller bar of lanoline, a white rock and a bottle of lager beer he'd brewed himself. He held up the lanoline, proudly:

'We haven't fixed the lather yet,' he said. 'People like a lot more lather in their lanoline. Stan is working on it in the lab. He's also using an artificial, imported perfume at present but would like to try out a local perfume from the trees or wild flowers of the bush. He'll go out one weekend with a group of local people and hunt out a new perfume. We want to turn people's attention to their natural resources. There aren't any local industries except corned beef, and if people only knew how and what to use from their surroundings we could become independent of the goods of the rich manufacturers in South Africa and Rhodesia.' He paused and held up the white rock. 'This is the Manyapiri stone. It is a source of lime for our buildings. We have started experiments in stonemasonry. We want to use the rocks of the bush for our project buildings. . . .'

He blinked uncertainly. His eyesight was not so good.

'Would you like to join the wool-spinning and weaving group?' he asked. 'My wife is organizing it.'

Before she could reply, his wife jumped up eagerly and from a table near by picked up a ball of wool and a ball of raw sheep's wool. Elizabeth hardly listened to the details of teasing, spinning and dyeing the wool. Two conflicting feelings rose up in her with a suppressed rush of words. She wanted to say: 'I must get out of here. I am panic-stricken. My internal life is all awry, and when I'm assaulted there I'm broken. I've withstood a lot of external hardships, but I'm incapable of withstanding internal stress, not the abnormal kind that's afflicting me.'

Then there was Thoko's pumpkin. Thoko had returned a few days ago and given her a gift of a huge, swollen yellow pumpkin. She had cooked a portion of it and sat for some time simply admiring its vivid orange hue.

'I'd prefer any kind of work with crops,' she said.

He nodded: 'We have an area of about one acre for a vegetable garden to go along with the project,' he said. 'We are clearing out the thorn-bush, slowly, over the weekends, but we need someone to concentrate on duplicating some of the new methods we have introduced at the farm, in the village garden. Would you like to do that?'

A lot of other things clicked into place after that. She had some savings. There was the small patch of unused school ground outside the school fence. A small whitewashed house sprang into existence there, overnight, built by the builders' work-group of Motabeng Secondary School. A dusty brown road swept past the door. The bush slept all around, and at night the insects communed with their own selves in long, brooding, plaintive soliloquies. The deep, black midnight sky vibrated with a billion soft blue lights, and at dawn the sun arose like a majestic king thrusting one powerful golden arm above the flat horizon. Only the bush, the brown road, the insects, the stars and the yellow-gold dawn remained a tender, background symphony. There was no beauty or tenderness in her learning:

What is love?

Who is God?

If I cry, who will have compassion on me as my suffering is the suffering of others?

This is the nature of evil. This is the nature of goodness.

Thoko's pumpkin led her along a rough stony road, one mile into deep bush. Leafy, spreading trees shaded the road. Hidden in the tangle of trees were the farm-buildings of the farmer's youth-development work-group. At the approach to the farm was a big whitewashed, grass-roofed, dormitory for the students and, a stone's-throw away, the rondavel-shaped house of the English farm manager. He was so intensely reserved and aloof that no conversation ever went beyond his work and crops. Over a period Elizabeth gathered a little more information about him. It was rather dull. He was a Quaker. He told Elizabeth, when she was smoking a cigarette in the dairy, that she'd spoil the milk and cheese, and that smoking was one of the vices of life. He said he didn't like the lager beer Eugene brewed because there were an awful lot of drunkards in Botswana and he was encouraging it. He didn't like any music but the great choral music of the cathedral churches of England he had on tape. In fact, he was so oppressively conservative and goody-goody that it was almost an anticlimax to say that he was one of the greatest agricultural minds in the country. He spent all his time adapting agriculture to water-conservation methods and had acquired such tremendous fame as a Botswana researcher that he was a formidable personality to have dealings with.

As though he knew about Thoko's pumpkin being the main cause of Elizabeth's venture into agriculture, he was in the habit of replying to her every query with rude and sarcastic remarks. His attitude clearly said: 'Yes, insect, and what do you want now? Can't you see I'm a very busy man?'

Much more fascinating, weird, human, lavish and entertaining were the Danish families who made up the small group of disgruntled farm-instructors. The farm-project seemed to be totally supported by the Danish government and was set up on a grand scale. They built large, modern houses for the people they sent over and took care of every detail of their lives, down to the last ounce of petrol. But they also paid for an elaborate watering system in the vegetable garden and stocked the dairy with fancy Friesland cattle. The cause of general gloom among the Danes was that they were all university graduates in agriculture who found themselves teaching barely or totally illiterate Batswana students. The only requirement for joining the youth-development work-groups was a slight acquaintance with English. Otherwise genius would arise overnight. They did not believe this. They spent all their sunset hours of leisure denigrating their pupils. Apparently they had a high standard of culture and civilization in Denmark.

Yet here again the conservative Englishman had naturally solved a problem they perpetually moaned about. He had selected the most brilliant students, who quickly grasped scientific terms and formulas, and placed them in positions of responsibility over the others. They formed a second vanguard of teaching instructors, communicating in Setswana all the knowledge they had grasped ahead of the others. He never talked about the stupidity or illiteracy of the material he had to work with. The first day Elizabeth approached him he said:

'Go down to the garden. It's another mile away from here. You'll find Small-Boy in charge. He'll tell you everything you want to know about the new methods we have introduced here. He's one of the best trainees we have.'

The Englishman did all the right things through an impatience for progress. He lacked the humanity of the Eugene man who had originated the projects. In his pamphlet writing, the Eugene man totally blurred the dividing line between the élite who had the means for education and the illiterate who had none. Education was for all. He always turned up with something for *everyone*. In this respect, he was an African, not a white man, and the subtlety of it spread to his conduct in everyday life. She had spent a day in his house. At lunchtime a group of labourers had walked into his house and sat down at table with him. They were Batswana. They had picked up their spoons, quietly bent their heads and eaten their food in a humble manner. He was so identical with them in gesture and posture that, startled, Elizabeth thought: 'How is it his movements and gestures are so African? There's such a depth of knee-bending in him, it's an unconscious humility.'

It always helped, too, when people from other lands took note of the future greatness of the African continent. As it was a part of the Peace Corp programme for volunteers to live with village families for the purposes of learning Setswana, one such young girl had once remarked to Elizabeth:

'They make you feel like a queen. Your every need is catered for and attentively watched over. There is little to share but it is shared beautifully, so that even an offer of a glass of water seems to be an offer of the most expensive champagne. People here are kings and queens to each other. . . .'

That morning as she walked down the rough, shady road to the vegetable gardens seemed to Elizabeth the greatest adventure she was ever to undertake. It is impossible to become a vegetable gardener without at the same time coming into contact with the wonderful strangeness of human nature. Every man and woman is, in some way, an amateur gardener at heart and vegetables are really the central part of the daily diet. Even in desert countries they are obtained by hook or crook. Everyone also knows *something* about vegetables they are over-eager to impart to a harassed gardener – if their grandfather didn't grow a vegetable, then their aunt did. But half of it was the joy of walking around a plot shimmering with bright green leaves, an expression of wonder on their faces, their hands absent-mindedly reaching into their pockets and handbags for coins. Had it all really

started with Small-Boy and Camilla, the Dane? Camilla had
to be included even though she was a pain in the blessed
neck.

She pushed open the small gate at the entrance to the
garden. Three students tended it, bent down, silently absorbed in their work. They wore green overalls.

'Good-day gentlemen,' she called from the gate. 'Who is
Small-Boy?'

One of the students working at overturning the soil on a
plot straightened up and waved his hand. As she approached,
his face broke into an enchanting, Puck-like grin. He had
small, twinkling, friendly eyes and a small up-turned nose.
As was polite Setswana custom, greetings and introductions
were the most important thing.

'That's Kepotho,' he said, pointing to a young boy, bent
over, thinning a carrot bed. 'That's Dintle,' he said, pointing
to the other young boy crouched near a shade-house where
seedlings were made. Then he added, proudly: 'Dintle is
my best friend.'

They all shouted back a greeting and continued with their
work. Elizabeth said: 'My name is Elizabeth. Mr Grahame
sent me here to take notes. He said you would tell me everything. I should also like to do some practical work. You've
heard about the local-industries project Eugene is starting in
the village near the school? It has a vegetable garden, and
we want to copy some of the new methods you are using
here for the garden.'

He nodded: 'I'll talk while I'm working,' he said, and
continued turning the lush, heavily-manured soil with his
fork. Elizabeth sat down next to the plot and spread her notebook open on her knees. The air was alive with the tinkle
of gently-seeping water. Laid down the centre of each bed
were long lengths of perforated plastic pipes. Water tippled
out of each like minute waterfalls, in a continuous stream.
A maze of piping, like a jig-saw puzzle, linked stream to
stream throughout the garden. It was a garden that watered
itself the whole day long, once the central tap was turned
on. Next to Elizabeth was a bed of the most gigantic cabbage
she had ever seen in her life before. She stared in wonder at
the nearest, full-moon face.

'What variety of cabbage is this?' she asked Small-Boy.

'Giant Drumhead Early,' he said, importantly.

'But they are so big!' she said, astounded.

'Of course,' he said. 'We have everything here, in the right proportions, for vegetables. I think they like this garden, and our watering system. Gunner always says vegetables don't like being splashed all over with water every day.'

'Do they mind being eaten?' she asked, stupidly. Small-Boy made the vegetables sound human. He smiled back at her, as one would at an idiot.

'They don't mind,' he said patronizingly. 'There's thousands of cabbage in a one-ounce packet of seed.'

She liked this sort of conversation, but Small-Boy took his work and position very seriously. He bent his head and started talking in the formal, severe way of a teacher.

'Once a bed has been used,' he said, slowly, 'and all the crops removed, I place three wheel-barrows of kraal manure on it and then broadcast one pound of chemical fertilizer in the proportions of two parts Nitrogen, three parts Phosphorus and four parts Potash ...'

He turned and pointed to the plot he was working on, where these basic preparations were complete.

'I need this bed again,' he continued, 'so I turn the soil once and deeply with a digging fork. I am careful to push the digging fork deep into the soil to the hilt, then turn. This way I ensure that enough soil mingles with fertilizer and manure, and they get down as deep as possible.'

He paused.

'The foundation of our garden,' he continued, 'is the deep trench bed. The use of it promotes quick growth and improves the quality of the vegetables. The following advantages for plants are also obtained; a good circulation of air in the bed and a strong root system, and you also conserve water. ...'

There was a sudden, jarring interruption from the gate. A woman's high, shrill voice swept over the garden. It was Camilla.

'Anyone playing dice around here?' she shrilled.

She came speeding towards them, her eyes, her hands, her walk creating a turmoil of distraction, shattering the sleepy, murmuring peace of the garden. All life had to stop and turn towards her. Her voice had an insistent command to it, yet it was no command of life. It was a scatter-brained assertion of self-importance. She stopped an instant at a bed and shouted to Small-Boy:

'Small-Boy! Didn't I tell you not to leave the manure on top of the bed? You must turn it in at once! The nitrogen evaporates.'

She sped around to where Elizabeth was seated on the ground.

'Ah!' she exclaimed, brightly. 'You must be Elizabeth. Grahame told me I'd find you here.'

She bent down and whipped the notebook out of Elizabeth's hand, ran her eyes down the page of notes and exclaimed: 'Ah, that, the deep trench garden,' whipped a pencil out of a pocket of her loose shift dress and rapidly began sketching something. She thrust the notebook back at Elizabeth. There were three parallel lines: One, surface. Two, dig-out. Three, substitute soil with manure. That dismissed the deep trench garden, irrespective of whether it was comprehensible to Elizabeth or not. She raced on:

'I assist Gunner who is class instructor,' she said. 'He is away on holiday at present. I'm really a landscape gardener in my own country. If someone doesn't come down here during practical work time these trainees will just sit under the trees and play dice. Come on, I'll show you the seedling preparation. It is one of the best methods of transplanting you can ever find. Grahame introduced it from South Africa. Isn't he a wonderful man? Ah!'

Elizabeth was forced to follow after her. She couldn't immediately collect her wits in this situation. The half-mad Camilla woman descended on Dintle, who had all along been filling small plastic bags with a soil preparation for seedlings. Under the shade-house were rows and rows of cabbage and tomato seedlings in plastic bags. She glanced at them and began shouting:

'Dintle! Why haven't you watered these seedlings? Tch! I don't understand these people!' She swung around on Elizabeth: 'You must be able to feel when plants need water. You must not wait to be told.'

All of a sudden, the vegetable garden was the most miserable place on earth. The students had simply become humiliated little boys shoved around by a hysterical white woman who never saw black people as people but as objects of permanent idiocy. She could not even begin to see the extreme delicacy and precariousness of the experiment, that they were young men who had had no future and were suddenly being given one, and that they took Eugene's offer very seriously. Knowing that Elizabeth was more literate than the students, she thrust her down too. She flung information at her in such a way as to make it totally incomprehensible and meaningless, subtly demonstrating that to reach her level of education Elizabeth had to be able to grasp the incoherent. She had a way of grasping the notebook out of Elizabeth's hands and scribbling her own notes, with sketches. She rushed about from one thing to another. It was really hatred at first sight, but the blue-eyed chattering woman seemed entirely unaware of it.

'God, I loathe her,' Elizabeth thought, struggling to find a way out of the garden as she was shouting at Small-Boy about a pipe that had burst and was wasting water.

'Wait a minute!' Camilla called. 'I'm going home too.'

Then she proceeded to dominate the rough stone road with its shady trees. Elizabeth was naturally an imbecile about the wonders of nature, and this Camilla had to make amends for on the mile-long journey to her home.

'Ah! That is my favourite tree! Just look at its buds! And the shape of it! Look! Look! Did you see that small grey mouse scampering into the bush? Ah! Isn't it wonderful! Look! Look! Did you see that bird? Grahame says it's called the Going-Away bird in Setswana. Don't you think that's charming?'

Elizabeth struggled to switch off the endless battery of chatter hitting her head and thought with adoring longing of the young boy, Small-Boy, who had started imparting information with an air of quiet, authoritative, manly calm. He had such a sure grasp of what he was saying and proceeded so methodically that she knew from the start he had a great teacher behind him. It must be the absent Gunner man.

'When is Gunner coming back?' she asked.

'He's away with his family in Denmark for three months,' said Rattle-tongue.

Elizabeth's heart fell to her boots. Three months was the period of her learning in the vegetable-garden. Was it going to be like this every day? Only Rattle-tongue?

They reached the turning-off pathway to her home.

'Come and have some tea,' said Rattle-tongue, with her ever-bright smile.

'Oh no,' said Elizabeth, hastily. 'I have to pick up my son at the nursery school. Then I want to check up on my house. The builders' work-group have nearly completed it. Then I have to catch the taxi at one o'clock back to Motabeng village.'

Camilla spread out her hands grandly. After all, she was here to help the natives and she couldn't miss this wonderful opportunity

'Here's my Landrover,' she said, pointing to the vehicle under a big tree. 'I can do all that for you in half an hour.'

Elizabeth looked at her with anguish. Human relationships with her were starkly black and white. She hated in a final way and loved in a final way. She had spent all her life running away from the type of white person like Camilla. They drew all the attention of life to themselves, greedily, hungrily. Her inner life was very dependent on the rightness of the inner life of another, and she had been wilting under the strain of Camilla's company. Half blindly, driven by the broiling heat of approaching summer, she accepted the offer. That clinched the bargain as far as Camilla was concerned. She threw herself with friendly intensity into an association with one of the natives. It was always there. Elizabeth's nativeness formed the background to all her comments. They ascented a steep pathway to a house built into the side of a small rocky hill. A stone stairway pieced together from the hill-side rocks led on to a wide entrance porch, then dropped again into another flight of stairs that led into a large sunken dining-room. It was so beautiful that Elizabeth gasped. Camilla had brought all her treasured household knick-knacks along with her. The lighting system was shaded with graceful Chinese lanterns; down one length of wall hung a calendar printed in bright red cloth with innumerable detail on its border edges about everyday life in a Danish village. Exquisite pale gold curtains swayed softly in the breeze. She was very fond of the colour red. Red couches, cushions and a brilliant carpet on the floor gave it an appearance of a flaming house of light.

'We liked the house so much that we extended our contract for a year,' she said. 'We were supposed to leave for Denmark last month.'

Elizabeth turned and stared at her incredulously. Houses were loved, not people. As soon as she had thrust a plate of rich, spicy cakes at Elizabeth, she turned on her favourite record:

'I don't understand these people. They don't know anything at all, and they're so lazy....'

It didn't require any comment from Elizabeth. It just went on and on. As she finally stopped the Landrover outside Elizabeth's mud hut in Motabeng village she said: 'Ah, I know where you live now. On Sunday I'll come and fetch you to supper.'

So jarring had the events of the previous day been that on the following morning, as she approached the tree under which was parked the white Landrover, Elizabeth stopped and peeped carefully around it. There was a little clearing ahead, then the protection of the shady trees. She couldn't endure the nature walk with Rattle-tongue. The whole front area of the house seemed deserted. She started across the clearing. Half way across she heard a shrill cry:

'Elizabeth!'

Camilla came running down the stone stairway. She was still tying up her hair into a bun, the buttons on her loose shift dress were undone.

'Elizabeth,' she panted. 'Why don't you wait for me? I've been keeping a look-out for you the whole morning. I thought: "Ah, she'll be along any time now. If she's early we can have a cup of tea, then walk down to the garden together." '

She looked so crazily, pathetically human that Elizabeth burst out laughing. Camilla nodded her head eagerly and laughed too.

'I have so many children,' she said. 'I'm always late in the morning because I have to dress after they've gone to school. There's no trouble with my husband. He's a farmer and up at five-thirty every morning.'

She swung into step beside Elizabeth and immediately began exclaiming on nature: 'Look!'

This veering in feeling – one minute she really loved the half-mad woman, the next, she loathed her – had a strange parallel in the notes she made in her notebook. The notes careered wildly between the calm, steady statements of Small-Boy and the erratic, incomprehensible outbursts of Camilla. The Sunday supper quickly gave Elizabeth the clue to this love for the incomprehensible in Camilla.

There was a whole crowd of Danes there, the specialists in sheep farming, dairy farming, crops and chickens. The talk centred on their culture and civilization and their disappointment at having to teach illiterates. At one point Camilla smiled, turned to Elizabeth and, momentarily dominating the conversation, said loudly:

'In our country culture has become so complex, this complexity is reflected in our literature. It takes a certain level of education to understand our novelists. The ordinary man cannot understand them ...'

She swung around for confirmation of this astounding event to a young girl seated in a withdrawn posture in a corner of the room. She was unmarried and a Maths teacher, come down from the secondary school.

'Birgette!' she said. 'You know something about this. You're the bookworm around here. There's a whole lot of novelists no one can understand. Their minds reflect the complexity of our culture. There's ...'

And she reeled off a list of authors, smiling smugly. It never occurred to her that those authors had ceased to be of any value whatsoever to their society – or was it really true that an extreme height of culture and the incomprehensible went hand in hand? Elizabeth looked with interest at the girl, Birgette. Up till then she had been so unobtrusive, so hidden, so silent as not to be noticed at all. She flinched at suddenly being made the centre of attention. She stared at Camilla with dark, unfathomable eyes, spread her hands out in a deprecating manner and said softly: 'I don't know anything about it.' And abruptly withdrew into her own shell. She was so blonde that her hair was snow-white. The short-cropped hair fell like a shaft of silk across her face as she turned her head and hid her face from view. That seemed to be the only centre of sanity in the babbling madhouse. Elizabeth stared, magnetically attracted to the hidden face. Camilla jumped up, touched her on the arm and whispered in her ear: 'Don't worry about Birgette. She's very shy and frightened of people.'

How strange was the network of human relationships at the Motabeng Secondary project! Because Elizabeth remembered the anguished face of the blonde girl, full of shadows as though she secretly endured an intolerable sorrow. She remembered a conversation with Small-Boy in the garden. Camilla was at the other end, shouting at Dintle and she had turned to Small-Boy and said: 'I don't like her. She just goes around saying people are stupid.'

'We know, and we don't like it,' Small-Boy said, angrily.

'It's not only her, the others who work here say the same thing.'

Small-Boy bent his head thoughtfully: 'You haven't met Gunner,' he said. 'He's the best man in the world. He loves people.'

She was to have a short and astonishing contact with the girl Birgette and a long and affectionate work-relationship with Gunner and come to an odd conclusion about Danes – they were either very, very bad or so impossibly God-like that they out-stripped the rest of mankind in humanity.

It was about a month later, once she had settled in her new home, that Elizabeth saw Birgette walk down the small brown road. It was sunset, and Elizabeth was busy in her garden, watering the small plots that surrounded the house. The girl stopped and smiled, then walked to the fence and peered over.

'There was nothing here a month ago,' she remarked. 'I passed this way and found only rock and stones and bush. And here you have a complete garden full of everything.'

'I've stolen some of the teaching work,' Elizabeth said. 'I have a group of women working with me and I've been teaching them to make seedlings in plastic bags. Then there was nowhere to plant them out because our garden in the valley still has to be fenced.'

'What are those?' Birgette asked, pointing to small, furry green bushes that lined the concrete footpath up to the front door.

'It's the Cape Gooseberry,' Elizabeth said. 'We're going to use the fruit for making jam.'

'Isn't it wonderful,' Birgette said. 'To know in advance that those small green bushes will eventually produce fruit for bottles and bottles of jam?'

Elizabeth laughed and shook her head: 'I don't know that yet. I can't see the jam, but Grahame can. He gave me the seed and said that the Gooseberry is one of the best fruits for jam.'

Birgette lifted her head, looked towards the door of Elizabeth's house and sniffed a little.

'There's something very nice cooking in there,' she said.

'It's a meat pie for supper,' Elizabeth said. 'Wouldn't you like to come in and share it? There's only my son and I, and the food's always more than we can eat.'

In contrast to her shy and shrinking air, she had a rapid, decisive way of walking. There was a lovely rhythm in her hips that made her skirt swirl out and sway around her as she walked. Her thick, silky white hair bounced up and down: 'I make all my decisions in a split second,' said her proud, serious face. 'And I know they're all noble. I have no other code of life.'

She pushed open the small gate, walked up the concrete pathway, stopped at the door and turned to stare at Elizabeth with a quiet attentive poise. She talked in movement and gesture: 'Life is such a gentle, treasured thing. I learn about it every minute. I think about it so deeply.'

So sensitively attuned was she to the feelings of others that Elizabeth nearly shouted out aloud with joy. The sun might go down and the stars come out. The beautiful girl in front of her was a part of that shift from light to shadow to darkness. She ran around the back of the house to turn off the garden tap. The small boy walked slowly home down the dusty brown road, lost in his own playtime thoughts. He crept quietly into the house behind them and squeezed himself into a corner. Apart from a whispered: 'Hello' to the visitor, not a word more did he utter.

'Why is he such a silent child?' asked Birgette.

'He isn't,' Elizabeth said, laughing. 'He's full of dangerous, top-secret information, but he won't part with it in the presence of strangers. He wanders into everybody's home and brings me back each day a detailed report of their doings. There's a terrible babble going on here each evening until he goes to bed.'

'You have a very pretty house,' Birgette said, looking around at the interior.

Almost everything in the house could be seen from the front door entrance. It was barely twenty feet in length. Three doors opened out, one on a small kitchen area in which was a sink and a stove, some shelves with plates and cups. A room on the right-hand side served as Elizabeth's bedroom. A room on the left served as a bedroom for the child, plus a dining-room. Directly opposite the front door entrance was a bathroom.

Birgette leaned against the kitchen sink as Elizabeth lit the candles and prepared the supper things.

'You are always in the company of Camilla,' she observed. 'Are you very fond of her?'

Elizabeth put the pie-dish on the sink and said, half-laughingly, half-vehemently: 'Am I always in her company, or is she always in mine? The silly thing has so many false assumptions about life, I've never been able to get in a word about not liking her. She's stone-deaf and blind. She takes the inferiority of the black man so much for granted that she thinks nothing of telling us straight to our faces we are stupid and don't know anything. There's so many like her. They don't see the shades and shadows of life on black people's faces. She's never stopped a minute, paused, stood back and watched the serious, concentrated expressions of the farm students. There's a dismal life behind them of starvation and years and years of drought when there was no food, no hope, no anything. There's a magical world ahead of them with the despair and drudgery of semi-desert agriculture alleviated by knowledge. When people stumble upon magic they study it very closely, because all living people are, at heart, amateur scientists and inventors. Why must racialists make an exception of the black man? Why must she come here and *help* the black man with a special approach: ha, ha, ha, you're never going to come up to our level of civilization?'

Birgette folded her arms about her chest as though she had suddenly become very cold, and said in a voice quivering with fright:

'Southern Africa is very dangerous.'

What did she mean? Was it the only area in the world where truthful statements could be made about the white man's hatred of the black man because it was such an established and accepted thing here? She looked up at Elizabeth and said, strangely:

'I first volunteered to teach in Algeria, then I went home for a while. Friends I'd had refused to talk to me, as though I had acquired some contamination. I expect to lose a few more friends when I go back again. . . .'

She bent her head a little, thoughtfully searching the ground with her eyes, then looked up at Elizabeth and said accusingly:

'Why don't you tell Camilla she's a racialist? You ought to tell her.'

Elizabeth was so taken off guard by this unexpected statement that she started guiltily. How did it work out in real life? Did one really go around saying to any white man or woman: 'You are a racialist'? Where would it end? One would go stark, raving mad if a deep and endless endurance of suffering, such as one could encounter in Southern Africa, were really brought to the surface. Subterraneously it was a powerful willing of the total extinction of the white man. He aroused a terrible hatred.

'They know,' she said, helplessly. 'They know they are racialists. If I really had to tell her what I think I'd jump up and strike her such a hard blow in the face she'd fall down stone dead at my feet.'

The young girl jerked her head to one side with a quick, decisive movement: 'All right,' she said, firmly. 'I'm going to tell her. I'll go and tell her she's a racialist. I'll go and tell her everything you said.'

Elizabeth stared at her, fascinated. She loved, more than anything, the wild, free, devil-may-care gesture, and truth was so often devil-may-care.

'Thank you,' she said, gently. 'No one's ever thought of that before, at least, not in my experience. The victim of a racial attitude cannot think of the most coherent and correct thing to do to change the heart of evil. He can scare them with violence. He can slaughter them; but he isn't the origin of the poison. It's like two separate minds at work. The victim is really the most flexible, the most free person on earth. He doesn't have to think up endless laws and endless falsehoods. His jailer does that. His jailer creates the chains and the oppression. He is merely presented with it. He is presented with a thousand and one hells to live through, and he usually lives through them all. The faces of oppressed people are not ugly. They are scarred with suffering. But the torturers become more hideous day by day. There are no limits to the excesses of evil they indulge in. There's no end to the darkness and death of the soul. The victim who sits in jail always sees a bit of the sunlight shining through. He sits there and dreams of beautiful wonders. He loses his children, his wife, his everything. What happens to all those tears? Who is the greater man – the man who cries, broken by anguish, or his scoffing, mocking, jeering oppressor?'

Birgette stirred a little, smiled, turned and placed both hands softly on the kitchen sink: 'You say everything I have in my own heart,' she said. 'But I cannot express myself so well because I have never suffered. I see suffering. It hurts me.' She paused and swayed towards Elizabeth, confidingly. 'I want to tell you something. My contract is over. I leave next week for Denmark, but I am disturbed. I always sit up every night reading before I go to bed, but I haven't been able to do so for the past few nights. My emotional disturbance prevents me from concentrating. I sit for hours with a book on my lap. My heart is crying, and I don't know why. . . .'

Then she staggered back a little as though alarmed that she had confided a terribly important secret. Elizabeth could think of nothing to say, except that they were alike; but she was so lonely, so self-contained, so wrapped up in her own isolation.

'I thought it must be Motabeng Secondary School and all we do here,' Birgette added. 'It's a particular dream of a particular man, catering for freaks. People who think of others before themselves are freaks. The world is full of hatred. . . .'

Almost blindly Elizabeth moved to set the food and plates on the table. The strength of the other woman, the stripped-down simplicity of her goodness, the split-second decisions on what was the most noble thing to do were like the proverbial straw flung at a drowning man. She was terrified of her own inner turmoil, the invasion of beastly things into her heart, mind and soul.

'God isn't a magical formula for me,' she burst out, 'God isn't a switched-on, mysterious, unknown current I can turn to and, by doing so, feel secure in my own nobility. It's you I feel secure about, strangely, as though we will encounter each other again in some other life and nothing would have shaken your nobility. But mine, my destiny is full of doubt, full of doom. I am being dragged down, without my willing, into a whirlpool of horrors. I prefer nobility and goodness but a preference isn't enough; there are forces who make a mockery of my preferences.'

Elizabeth paused. The young girl looked up at her with intent seriousness and quiet awareness.

'I imagine a situation in some future life,' Elizabeth continued. 'I imagine my face contorted with greed and hatred. I imagine myself wilfully grabbing things that are not mine. And in this darkness of the soul, you will one day walk up to me and remind me of my nobility. That will be my magical formula. I'll hear you and turn away from the darkness. Will you do that for me?'

Without pausing to consider the matter, Birgette nodded her head and said: 'I will.'

Elizabeth laughed. She was a cringing jellyfish scared of her intangible perceptions of a Medusa, of a Sello in a brown suit. Their concerted evil was so powerful, it threw her flat on her back. The roots of evil, as a creative, propelling force, had become as close as her own breathing. And what had Sello been in her earlier perceptions – a God?

'Something happened to me here,' she said. 'It was the total de-mystifying of all illusions. The human soul is alone in the battle of life. It is helped, I think, by profoundly moral social orders, such as Moses established for the Jews. But at best they can only be outer guide-lines, outer reminders. The questions of tenderness, love, appeal, compassion, truth, still lie within. I can be destroyed.'

Birgette shook her head a little. 'I sense something in your argument that does not apply to my own life,' she said. 'You might not realize it, but you are placing a tremendous importance on your own life. I have never felt that way about myself. My vision is limited to my preoccupations. I could tell you all of them. I read. I work. I travel. And I don't fall in love.'

That of course made the conversation veer towards love. Like the young girl opposite her, Elizabeth had no experience of love, but she had powerful imaginings about it; its quality and beauty were like a deep, hidden symphony in her heart.

'There's something haunting me,' she said, slowly. 'A past where I loved many people, but the quality of that love was so high, the memories, the images have a way of floating towards me with soft, undemanding faces. The shadowy figures seem merely content to put themselves in my arms and go to sleep, with complete trust: Here I am secure. Here I am safe. I have a peculiar sensation of sleeping with a whole lot of people in my arms, like a great and eternal mother. I thought: Love is so powerful, it's like unseen flowers under your feet as you walk. . . .'

As she said the last lines, the girl Birgette turned her head towards her own heart with deep, sad eyes as though it had begun crying again.

There was a short sequel to that lovely evening. Two days later Elizabeth met Camilla. She met a totally changed woman with a soft, subdued air, as near as a woman of her type could ever come to brooding reflection. She stared at Elizabeth for a while with wide, enquiring blue eyes. She raised one hand and said in a casual, offhand way: 'I told you in the beginning that vegetable gardening isn't really my line. I'm a landscape gardener in my own country.'

They walked down together to the vegetable garden. Camilla no longer exclaimed about nature. She walked quietly between the plots, and the small waterfalls tinkled softly. The students bent their heads in deep concentration on their work.

The year ended in a roar of pain. Sudden and terrible head-aches descended on her. She lost track of the details of that period. None of the images and pictures of Medusa or Sello were retained, nor their activities together. It was like a black, roaring sea of obscenity, on the high tide of which Medusa rose and stared down at her from an immense height. By day, Elizabeth crawled around, painfully. By night she lay back, a pinned-down victim of approaching death. Medusa had the air of one performing a skilled and practised murder. She seemed to say to herself:

'I'll let loose another bolt here. I'll let loose another bolt there. Ahah, look how she topples over!'

It wasn't Elizabeth's body she was thrusting into extinction. It was the soul; the bolts were aimed at her soul. It seemed to make death that much slower, that much more piecemeal. The narrow, mean eyes of Sello in the brown suit stared at her over Medusa's shoulder. In the roar of approaching con-fusion of mind, Elizabeth thought:

'I ought to get someone to take care of my son for me. He does not have to die with me.'

At the nursery school they had taught her son to make paper aeroplanes, boats and cars. His whole life was absorbed in these things. But Medusa had thought out a solution to the problem. She looked at Elizabeth and said calmly: 'You know you are going to die. The day you die you must take your son with you, because we don't want him here either.'

They stared at each other, lost in a death-grip struggle. Elizabeth fell back into death. The dawn arose one day, a week before Christmas. She remained in bed, dimly staring at the early sunlight. Suddenly someone knocked at the door. She crawled out of bed. A woman of about Elizabeth's own age stood at the door. Her name was Kenosi. She belonged to the wool-spinning and weaving group of the local industries project, but on several occasions had worked with the garden group allocated to Elizabeth. There was something wrong with the project. People peered at it, joined a work-group for a week, then ran away. It demanded solid voluntary work with no financial rewards, and the very poor whom it was to cater for did not care to work for no money. After about three weeks Elizabeth had no one working with her, except Kenosi. She had asked Kenosi to join the garden group and been given a flat, severe refusal:

'No,' Kenosi had said. 'I prefer the wool work.'

She was the sort of woman who simply ate up all the work in front of her, with a deep silence and concentration. There was a wonderful majesty and purposefulness about her, like the way cats go about their daily affairs. She walked with a soft tread, lifting her feet clear off the ground the way cats do, and nodded her bent head in rhythm with her walk, the way cats do. The outer expression of her face was permanently severe and she had a way of lifting her head and staring at a person, with an inscrutable expression that might be distrust or might be a secret summarizing of human nature.

'What is it?' Elizabeth asked, suppressing a cry of pain; her head was reeling. 'Do you want something?'

'I have come to join you in the work,' Kenosi said.

Elizabeth swayed a little. The pain in her head eased.

'Come in,' she said.

The small boy was seated on the floor, busy with a paper aeroplane. As Kenosi entered, he looked up and immediately engaged her in the intricacies of his invention. It was a way of village life, he had learned. Children were caressed and attended to, their conversations were listened to with affectionate absorbtion. As Kenosi sat down, he stood up, pushed against her lap and put his aeroplane in her hands. They began an animated discussion in Setswana, excluding Elizabeth. The distraction had brought her back to life; Elizabeth laughed and put on a kettle for tea, washed and dressed.

Half an hour later they all walked down to the site of the local-industries project. Across the brown dusty road, a pathway led down into a wide valley area in which no one lived.

There were a few clusters of tall trees. Winding through the valley was a small, dry stream-bed. Running parallel to the dry stream was the one-acre area of the garden. Surrounding the garden were the partly-erected work buildings of the project; a brewery, a pottery house, the foundations for a kitchen, weaving house, wash-room and toilets and the partly-erected walls of a large shop that was to house and distribute the goods they produced. The site was deserted. Everyone had taken off for the holiday period over Christmas and New Year. Lying within the garden area were sixty poles waiting to be erected for the garden fence. Some men had dug holes right round the circumference of the garden.

Kenosi and Elizabeth picked up a pole at either end and placed it in a hole. They filled the hole around the pole with stones and Elizabeth hung on to the pole while the other woman wedged them in firmly with a crowbar. They smoothed the top over with soil. By midday they had set in six poles. Elizabeth clung to the woman. There seemed to be no other justification for her continued existence, so near to death was she.

'Let us go and eat at my house,' she said at lunchtime.

Without a word, Kenosi padded softly alongside her. The small boy took up the rear. He had a box under his arm in which he carried all his paper inventions of the morning. No one spoke. It did not occur as odd to either Elizabeth or Kenosi that they had both suddenly started working so hard when everyone else had gone away on holiday. As far as Elizabeth was concerned she was to look back on this strange week and the Kenosi woman's sudden appearance as one of the miracles or accidents that saved her life.

No other woman so strikingly resembled a cat in all her gestures. Her movements were extraordinarily quiet, soft, intensely controlled. Out of the corner of one eye Elizabeth watched, utterly fascinated, as she ate her food. She broke it up into small pieces and put it daintily into her mouth with the fork. Then she made distinct, sucking noises as she chewed, the way cats do. She kept herself severely wrapped up in herself, her eyes bent down towards her plate. It was three days before Christmas. By way of conversation, Elizabeth asked:

'How do you spend Christmas day?'

'I am a Roman Catholic,' Kenosi replied, without looking up. 'In the night before Christmas, I foot it into Motabeng with my friends for midnight mass at the church. On Christmas Day I attend a feast. There is always someone slaughtering a cow. They tell people, then we all go and eat at this person's house. This year we hear it will be the shop-owner of the village. Last year it was the owner of the garage. It is very nice. They play music and people dance. I go with my friends early in the morning to help the wife with the cooking. How do you spend it?'

'I'm going to make a cake for my son and I have a chicken to roast,' Elizabeth said, very put out at this meagre way of spending Christmas.

'You don't spend it with anyone?' Kenosi asked, surprised.

'I have no friends,' Elizabeth said.

'Where is the husband?' she asked, pointedly.

'I don't know,' Elizabeth said. 'One day I walked out of the house and never saw him again.'

Kenosi looked up quietly from her plate and fixed her inscrutable stare on Elizabeth. She kept her thoughts absolutely to herself.

'Are you married?' Elizabeth asked.

'No.'

'Is it difficult to find a husband?' Elizabeth persisted.

'Yes.'

'Do you have any children?'

'I have one child,' she said.

She was really an exceedingly beautiful woman in strength and depth of facial expression, in knowingness and grasp of life; its sorrows, its joys, its expected disillusionment. She was really the super-wife, the kind who would keep a neat, ordered house and adore in a quiet, undemonstrative way both the husband and children.

'If I were a man I'd surely marry you,' Elizabeth said gaily.

It was the first time Kenosi smiled. The edges of her eyes crinkled up with a deep humour. She put her fork down, momentarily, and placed both hands softly on the table.

'I work with my hands,' she said, proudly. 'I have always worked. I do any kind of work.'

The small boy had been listening to the conversation with bright, intent eyes. Caught up in the rhythm of her statement, he unconsciously put his hands on the table and mimicked: 'I work with my hands. I have always worked. I do any kind of work.'

Elizabeth never liked him mimicking her. She looked at him crossly and said: 'My God, this child is very bad.'

Wickedly he repeated: 'My God, this child is very bad.'

Again, there it was, the pretty, crinkling smile of deep humour. It was so brief, so carefully parted with that all the power of her personality seemed to depend on severity and reserve.

They walked down to the garden in the valley once more. It was broiling hot. No rain had come that summer. There wasn't even a promise of it in the starkly blue, molten sky. Like a stunned robot, Elizabeth worked beside the woman. The small boy set himself down under a big tree and continued working on his inventions. As the sun set, like a blaze of hellfire on the horizon, they parted. Kenosi turned once, clasped both hands together, made a short curtsey and said: 'Thank you for the food,' then padded quietly away to her home in the distance. A crashing depression descended on Elizabeth. She pushed her leaden feet towards the small boy who sat under the tree. He was completing his thousandth aeroplane. She took a packet of cigarettes and a box of matches out of her dress pocket. She handed him the box. He always lit the cigarette.

'If I die, would you like to die too?' she asked, crazily.

'What is to die?' he asked, interested.

She kept quiet a moment. It was very difficult to explain. He hadn't seen any dead thing yet for a concept to be formed in his mind.

'It's like going away,' she said. 'There isn't anyone to cook food or wash clothes. The house gets empty.'

'Where do we go to?' he asked, a little anxiously.

'I don't know,' she said.

He immediately lost interest in the subject. He had once taken a train journey to another village, and sat bolt upright the whole way with wide alert eyes, silently absorbing all the sights. It was clear in his mind that she had no particular plan this time, that she was talking idly, that there was no suitcase to pack.

What did mothers, black mothers, say to children whose fathers had been lynched by the Ku Klux Klan in America? She had a picture of a Southern lynch mob, a whole group of white men and women. Two black men hung dead from a tree. The lynchers were smiling. Medusa smiled like that in her mental images, but Medusa was as close as her own breathing, and each night she looked straight into Medusa's powerful black eyes. It was tracing the evil to its roots. The eyes of the lynch mob were uncomprehendingly evil. Medusa's eyes were full of comprehension, bold, conscienceless, deliberate: 'I will it. Nothing withstands my power. I create evil. I revel in it. I know of no other life. From me flows the dark stream of terror and destruction.'

How much status had she not acquired during the dark times of mankind's history? How deep had she sown her seeds in the subconscious life of human souls? Wherever relentless cruelty and hatred erupted, it was like the dark geyser of Medusa's soul, erupting. Her followers were confused. She had not been identified, isolated from creative forces. They said they were worshippers of Jesus Christ and they lynched people; they committed so many atrocities.

That night Medusa and Sello in the brown suit were engaged in an eager whispering conversation. At one point Medusa turned her head towards Elizabeth and smiled triumphantly. Sello was pointing to the figure of a man in the distance. She overheard him say to Medusa: 'Don't worry, he'll kill her.'

At this Medusa walked up to Elizabeth. She had in her hands one of her bolts. These bolts seemed to ooze out of her hands. She had a way of shaping them into round balls, raising her arms in a wide, swinging movement and hurling them straight at Elizabeth. They exploded against her like lightning bolts. She often slipped into black unconsciousness and awoke later with a roaring headache.

Medusa raised her arms: 'We are,' she said, spelling out

the words, slowly: 'We are bringing you the real magic, this time.'

Elizabeth raised one hand feebly in defence. She said: 'I can't stand any more of this. My health is failing.'

Medusa turned her head from side to side, smiling, indicating enchantment: 'Oh, but you will love it,' she said. 'Dan is so beautiful.'

Then she shaped her mouth into a yap: 'Here's the last of them,' and the black bolt came hurtling towards Elizabeth. It was about to explode in her face. She put both hands before her and jerked wide awake with a scream. She was trembling so violently that the bed shook. With no clear plan in her head, she pushed her legs out of the bed. As she tried to stand, they wobbled like rubber. She fell down on her knees and began crawling across the floor. The chair on which Sello, the monk, eternally sat, was in her son's room. She crawled to the chair and looked up. She could clearly discern the outline of his form in the white cloth.

'Sello,' she groaned painfully. 'Find another punch-bag for your girl. I'm not her match.'

'All right,' he said, quietly.

She turned to crawl back to her bed. A billowing wave of darkness rose up and sucked her to its depths, and she sank to the floor.

When she opened her eyes it was daylight. Her son was lying on the floor beside her and peering into her face.

'Why are you sleeping on the floor?' he asked seriously.

She couldn't think of anything to say and kept quiet.

'What was you burning last night?' he asked, pointing to her room. 'The floor is full of burnt things.'

She jumped up alarmed. Why, anything could happen in her nightmare. She might have left a cigarette lit. She walked to the door of her bedroom, then froze. There was the drama of a death-throe on the floor. Charcoal-like foot-prints dragged into each other across the floor and in the centre of the room was a heap of charcoal dust. She half muttered aloud to herself:

'Is this the last of Medusa?'

From the room behind her Sello said: 'Yes.'

'What are you saying?' the small boy asked.

'Poetry,' she said. She had found that the word 'poetry' excused any mental ramblings and he understood. He was supposed to say Jack and Jill went up the hill, out loud. She said it was all poetry, only hers was complicated.

He was disturbed. He stood looking up at her. Odd events – and his mother was capable of producing many – usually entertained him. But what was she doing on the floor? She thrashed about in her mind for an explanation. To her relief there was a knock on the door. It was Kenosi again to 'join her in the work'.

'Hello,' Elizabeth said, smiling.

She returned the greeting, unsmiling, severe. They stared at each other. Kenosi raised her head, speculatively. A wave of thought passed over her face. It clearly said: 'If you think your smile is an indication of the possibilities of friendship between us, then I must tell you that I'm the sort of person who studies people first.'

But as soon as the small boy poked his head out beside Elizabeth, Kenosi immediately turned to him and smiled, tenderly. He eagerly thrust a paper aeroplane at her.

'It's a jet,' he said.

She took it, still smiling. Apparently people here made sharp distinctions between adults and children, and hostilities were restricted to adults.

'Is it a gift?' she asked.

'It's got to go in the sky,' he said indignantly.

Elizabeth was still in her nightdress.

'I haven't cleaned my house up yet,' she said. 'But come inside.'

Kenosi shook her head: 'I'll sit here till you are ready,' she said. And she turned and seated herself on the ground near the door. The small boy climbed into her lap.

She could hear them chattering outside as she swept up the charcoal dust, made the bed and prepared to wash and dress. The small boy's voice had become weighty and important. He was really an engineer bowed down under the problems of his construction works:

'They tell me a lot about aeroplanes at school,' he observed. 'They say jets go faster than any other aeroplane.'

'Yes,' Kenosi said.

'I'm afraid about what happens when my jet comes to the edge of the earth,' he said. 'It will fall right off.'

'Yes,' Kenosi said.

'Do you think it's better then that I fly it about in the middle?' he asked anxiously.

'Yes,' she said.

'I'm afraid of the edge,' he said. 'I think a lot of things have fallen off the edge. The edge is where the sun comes up. And the other edge is where the sun goes down. I asked my mother if that was the edge and she said yes. The goats keep on going to the edge and falling off. My mother says once they fall off they just keep on falling and falling because there is no bottom. I can never go far away from home in case I fall off too.'

She heard Kenosi giggling loudly.

All day long they worked at setting up the poles in the garden, and at evening these stood like silent sentinels, except for the empty spaces of the corner-posts and gate-posts which had to be set in with cement for added strength. As on the previous day, just before departing, Kenosi turned, clasped two hands together, made a curtsey and said: 'Thank you for the food.'

All day long, Elizabeth had brooded. There was a blinding sense of light and liberation in her head. She had hung over a cliff of death and obliteration and had been flung back into life again. It was a life that flowed softly, with its own slow, weaving, gentle pattern. In the death in which she had lived, she had been totally forced to pay attention to the dominant, raucous demands of Medusa. It did not matter there if flowers grew or women had children. Nothing mattered but the power of Medusa and her plans. She was aware that Sello had been manipulating Medusa's words and gestures and studying their effects on Elizabeth. He had defined the future, in African terms, as one of uncompromising goodness. It had been fixed for her securely in his earlier attitudes. Then he had tried to weave Medusa into this structure. She was too powerful a personality for his methods: the slow, interweaving pattern of life where one thing influenced another, where cells formed and re-formed in a natural way without violence. Why did he display only that aspect of Medusa? Why had he occupied himself all the time with evil?

As she walked home, Elizabeth raised her hands to her head. Her whole head was scarred in deep grooves of pain. She had seen nothing explicit in hell; the pictures had jumped at her and returned to obscurity. Sello had not really shared any of his perceptions with her. Each thing had come to her as a backwash of obscenity. It was the implications in Medusa's words and gestures that had run along those grooves in her head as though she were saying: 'Now I know the feeling of deep perversion. It is shameful. It is acts demented people perform in dark, hidden places. It makes one ashamed to have legs.'

This very suggestiveness, of dark, deep secrets, had made everything more terrible to endure than the actual sight of the horror.

She could see in his attitude that evening that an episode of the inner life was over. He turned to her and said, with a quiet despair: 'You don't realize the point at which you become evil.'

He sat with his arms hanging listlessly in his lap. He was reduced to a quarter of his former size, so shrunken that his monk's cloth flapped about his form like a scarecrow's rags. A strange drama unfolded behind him. He paid no heed to it, staring ahead straight into the future with forlorn eyes. The mystical madonna moved into focus again. She still sat with her long hair flowing around her like a wet mat and fixed her abstracted gaze on nothing. Out of the darkness, a man quietly approached her. He wore a white cloth, like Sello, but he kept his hands clasped in front of him as though his life were a constant prayer. He paused for a while and stared at Elizabeth with wide, round eyes. She wasn't sure if he wanted to smile or communicate in some way, but the feel of his personality was one of extreme gentleness and tenderness. From beside the mystical madonna he picked up a crown and placed it on her head. It was unlike the crowns worn by 'the Father' or the wife of Buddha. Those had glowed with an unearthly light. The crown he gave her resembled that of earthly queens. He looked up again, this time towards Sello, and his face crumpled as though he were about to cry.

'Who are you?' Elizabeth asked on an impulse.

He kept on looking at Sello: 'He knows,' he said. 'He knows how long I have loved her, in silence. He knows me. He knows how long I have loved him too.'

As Elizabeth turned to Sello, he pointed to an area that glowed with light. It was the opening of the cesspit he had once shown her. She stared down it. It was like a crater that had opened up in the earth, and so deep, so endless was the fall to the bottom of it that it seemed bottomless. It was quite clean and empty now, so much so that its jagged stone walls seemed to be made of marble, yet it might only have been the effect of light. It was full of light. As she stared down it, a shape formed and eased itself up out of the hole. As it fell in a heap outside the hole, she recognized her bath-towel. The prolonged staring into the depths made a wave of dizziness overcome her. She began to pitch over into the hole. As she slipped over the edge, she clung to its periphery with both hands, her legs dangling down into the pit. Alarmed, she cried out: 'Oh God, if anyone plans evil like this again, may they suffer alone and not involve others. If anyone has to fall, let them fall alone.'

Immediately, her feet found a grip in the jagged side of the rock and she climbed out. She sat trembling a little at the side of the hole. A loud, slithering noise reached her ears. There seemed to be an endless procession of dead bodies, flat on their backs. One after the other they pitched in until the hole was full. She had brief glimpses of their faces as they hurtled past her. They were the people she had briefly seen in hell, who had jumped on the bandwagon of wilful evil. They pitched in and pitched in until the hole was filled to the brim. Among the dead bodies lay Caligula, stick legs, the strutting emperor of heaven.

She awoke and stared around her. The phosphorescent glow of her clock hands indicated three o'clock. A full moon was shining outside. She opened the door and looked out on the still, flat, moonlit earth. The thorn-trees and mud huts, black shadows in the night, seemed that much more deeply asleep on the quietly glittering earth. How did it all happen here, in so unsuspecting a climate, these silent, tortured, universal questions of power and love; of loss and sacrifice? What did all those dead bodies mean? She was startled to hear Sello say quite clearly:

'If you did not like anything, I destroyed it. It was alive, that body of deep evil from so long ago, it was still alive. I destroyed it all.'

It couldn't be that simply put. He had placed her in the pathway of his madonna. It had nearly cost her her life and sanity. Such are the times of exalted moods, when one thinks a sacrifice or great gesture is complete, that she turned with a stirring of deep admiration to Sello and thought: 'He has done something great. Who could sit and look on their own pus-oozing sores for so long? And he hasn't only the record of darkness behind him. He created light as well.'

She underestimated the wounds inflicted by Medusa, her overriding arrogance, and the depths of her perversion which she paraded as desirability; nor did she gauge how much suppressed contempt she felt for the man Sello, who had been totally dominated by an evil woman. Too often the feelings of a victim are not taken into account. He is so disregarded by the torturer or oppressor that for centuries evils are perpetrated with no one being aghast or put to shame. The tempo of it had been speeded up, brought breath-close and condensed to a high-pitched ferocity. It rumbled beneath her consciousness like molten lava. It only needed someone to bring the hot lava to the surface for her to find that a process of degradation, scorn and wild, blind cruelty had its equivalent of wild, savage vengeance in her.

But that night, as she brooded on the logic of goodness alone, she seemed to think it justified suffering: 'Yes,' she thought. 'He has performed some delicate operations. He has seen that evil and good travel side by side in the same personality. He has diagnosed the evil, isolated it and ended it. There's no more Medusa.'

Hadn't they a name for her in India – Mahamaya, the Weaver of Illusions, the kind that trapped men in their own passions? It was the trap of death. They had stumbled upon her as a creative force, as a power outside themselves that could invade and destroy them. They had performed delicate mental disciplines about an evil never personified, but they had vividly personified God. He had become more real, and Satan a shadowy indistinct blur of bad things. And yet at one time, now lost in myth, Satanic powers had been vividly a part of social orders. Something was eluding her – the mystical madonna. How had all her wild fires quieted down into that still river of eternal abstraction of soul? She reflected on those times, also lost in myth, where vague memories had lingered of the wars of the Gods. A warrior like Perseus had appeared to cut off the head of the terrible gorgon; there had been so much slaughter to bring destructive powers under control. Elizabeth could only speculate. Perhaps at some dim time Medusa had encountered Perseus and, out of the death he had inflicted on her, risen again with a still, sad, fire-washed face. She had only the record Sello had shown her of his own rise from Caligula to Osiris, the man free of any dominance by women.

There was something more elusive still: Sello's African circumstances. He had half-indicated great resources of strength and goodness in his surroundings. Or what did the poor mean by: Take off your vesture garments? Did they, as the victims of those who had everything, also see into the nature of a soul like Sello's? That was what he seemed to do that whole year, until he had no vesture garments left. Humility, which is a platitude of saints and recommended for the good life, could be acquired far too drastically in Africa.

And still something eluded her. She understood the basic teaching methods of goodness. They led the heart and mind on bit by bit; they appeared to resolve impossible conflicts. He was saying something else this time about the crying in the heart, that love-relationships are like an eternal damnation – they unfold and fulfil themselves, and the deeply drawn links of soul to soul have to be discarded. It was that which was impossible and almost never achieved, certainly not with the quivering, ecstatic beauty of a madonna. The heart was crying for that beauty, that perfection. Raw passions had never been admissible in those relationships, but when the mind of the monk was turned down towards earthly things he became a grotesque murderer. The ethereal loves bind soul to soul with chains that shatter death, physical distances or any other obstacle. An unfortunate victim who intrudes into this mystical union is ruthlessly slaughtered.

'I'll strangle it to death with evil,' he seemed to say throughout that long year. Because at the end of it – the hideous display of Medusa's power – he sat in death, incapable of thought, feeling, movement. Elizabeth was not a part of his death, nor had she really felt that crying in the heart. She had been forcefully thrown into a state of death, alongside Sello, battered and smashed about, but she instantly sprang to life again, laughed and flung her hands into the air with a bounding sense of liberation.

The dawn came. The soft shifts and changes of light stirred with a slow wonder over the vast expanse of the African sky. A small bird in a tree outside awoke and trilled loudly. The soft, cool air, so fresh and full of the perfume of the bush, swirled around her face and form as she stood watching the sun thrust one powerful, majestic, golden arm above the horizon.

'Oh God,' she said, softly. 'May I never contribute to creating dead worlds, only new worlds.'

PART TWO

DAN

SAY a warrior takes on any kind of battle because war is his business. It is an ugly business but, like all activities, it forms its own moral codes so that the business may be conducted as nobly as possible. In some depth of his soul the warrior is defending social values that he assumes his enemy lacks. All the same, the character and quality of his enemy is exposed during battle. They both present the other with death, but should the enemy turn out eventually to be a noble man in himself, he loves him. Somewhere at the back of her mind Elizabeth, though a woman, lived by the general's code. She formulated her own broad definition of it. Never wage war on an inferior. He is a rat who pulls too many dirty tricks. He starts a war he never intends ending. He entangles the soul in deceit till all codes are lost, all nobility degraded, till all of life is tainted with his slime. Throw down the weapons and walk away. And if he creeps up and stabs you in the back, die.

He came along from out of nowhere. He came along from outer space. He came along in clouds of swirling, revolving magic, with such a high romantic glow that the whole of earth and heaven were stunned into silence before the roar of his approach. One moment she had sat lost in brooding reflection on all the enigmas of the soul, quietly mending the raw ends of her shattered nervous system, the next a terrible clamour engulfed her life. Only on thinking back did she realize that it was the clamour of a man laughing his pissing head off. He had everything arranged in advance. He knew exactly what he wanted. He knew exactly what he was doing. He knew exactly who was going to die and how he was going to pick up the thirty pieces of silver at the end of the job. He was in it for money. The things of the soul were the greatest money-spinning business on earth. Treasures in heaven could be turned into real cash.

There was this feeling of overwhelming wealth and power; he produced the sort of concentrated atmosphere that had

made mystics fall to their feet in frightened awe and ex-
claim: 'Woe is me. I have seen the glory of the Lord.' He
assembled his soul and form in a wide, sweeping arc over
heaven and earth. One half of him seemed to come shooting
in like a meteor from the furthest end of the universe, the
other rose slowly from the depths of the earth in the shape
of an atomic bomb of red fire; the fire was not a cohesive
flame, but broken up into particles of fine red dust. All put
together it took the shape of the man, Dan. Again, the
details of the living man were scant. He was one of the very
few cattle millionaires of the country. He ordered a fantastic
array of suits from somewhere, and he was short, black and
handsome. He was the friend of Sello, so people said. Someone told her he was also greatly admired for being an African
nationalist in a country where people were only concerned
about tribal affairs. Otherwise the circle of people he moved
amongst were so removed from the sorts of people she associated with as to make his way of life a total mystery. They
were frighteningly scornful and aloof, and generally wore
dark glasses. Sello belonged in that circle too.

Dan was the kind of man she would never have looked at
till doomsday. It was much worse from her side, she wasn't
a genuine African; she was a half-breed. Dan was later to
inform her: 'People don't care a damn about you. They're
worried about the prophecies. It's this God thing.'

She stood at the window that evening watching the
assembly of his elemental soul. It was in an open space, then
the form of the man walked to her house. Alarmed, she
jumped up and rushed to the door. Sello had produced no
such phenomena; she had grown accustomed to seeing things
in pictures and imagery, but she had not seen such a
spectacular display of soul-power. The man walked right in
the door and brushed past her. She caught a glimpse of his
face. It was set in a grim line, his forehead was a frown of
concentration. He walked with a quick, firm, determined
stride.

'Who are you?' she asked, frightened.

He did not reply. She meant his soul-name. People's souls
walked right into her. It had been going on for some time.
They were all keepers of tender things that they loved as

though there were indeed such things as a God of the flowers, of spring, summer, autumn, winter; of family life; of children; of animals; of birds, and as though there were kings like 'the Father' who was the God of the poor man.

She turned around and stared at the man. She was so taken off guard by this sudden development that her wits totally deserted her. She was entirely dependent on what he would do, and what he did was astonishing. He bent right down to the floor and kissed her toes. As he removed his mouth a warm glow remained on the area he had touched. It changed the atmosphere drastically. How long had it gone on, the impersonal philosophical ramblings of Sello, and for how long had she watched quite close up the shameful display of Sello, the woman dominated effeminate slob, peeping round the skirts of Medusa? More than anything, the extreme masculinity of the man instantly attracted her. This he quickly noted. There was a rush of confidences.

'My darling,' he said, brokenly. 'I've been here for some time. I've watched over everything.'

That was the only truthful thing he ever said, that he knew everything. He never said he was going to use all his insight for his own ends. Apparently Sello had let him in on everything. He had viewed, along with Sello, the length and breadth of Sello's degradation in the dark times. Here was a situation indeed, a prophet with prophecies having such a dark past. He wasn't sure about Elizabeth's attachment to Sello. He first fell into the role of the outsider, kindly including Sello, the monk, who sat silently on the chair, so indifferent in appearance he might have been totally absorbed in his own sorrows.

He said of Sello: 'He never gets born without them. The prophecies included you.'

What was she to make of this astounding information? He did not expand on the nature of the prophecies, nor did it occur to her to make any further enquiries. He moved towards her and grasped her firmly around the waist. Obviously he was going to kiss her. She clamped a hand across her mouth.

'You can't do that,' she said. 'We are strangers.'

Obviously she was in an easily invaded world, but the

events in it were controlled – as though it had to happen that Medusa should assault her, it had to happen that people should approach her, but the movements were impersonal, no one personally loved her or touched her in such a way as to invoke physical sensations. The man placed his mouth on her hand. The most exquisite sensation passed from him to her. She had no equivalent of it in herself; it was almost indescribable; it was warm, it vibrated, it was a heightened ectasy.

She debated a moment with herself: 'I ought to find out more about this.' She removed her hand.

He kissed as firmly and decisively as the way he had grasped her around the waist. This exquisite vibration seemed to make the atmosphere very exalted. There was an undertone totally unfamiliar to her. He made a woman feel like an ancient and knowledgeable queen of love. It ill fitted her pattern, it was the property of lanky, slinky, smouldering females. She did not immediately recognize the disadvantage, the effect it had on her, heightening her gawkiness and commonplaceness and thrusting her down to the position of one who is being given a supreme gift by one in a station or situation far removed from her. But he was quite satisfied with this arrangement. He said: 'Ah,' as though he had triumphantly acquired Pavlov's dog.

Again, he placed himself in the position of the outsider, just about to enter the door. He recalled another man, 'the Father', this time with the generosity one male displays to another male.

'He and I,' he said, 'have performed the same roles in your destiny. How often has he heard that cry for help? But how much more often have I?'

No details were ever to unfold of her past relationship with Dan, but they had already unfolded of her relationship with 'the Father'. This had made no direct, possessive impact on her mind because of his basic personality. It was icily impersonal, as though other preoccupations dominated over themes of love. Also he had been introduced to her by Sello entirely as a soul personality. Sello had made her understand that he had come to Motabeng at some stage, worked for the Motabeng Secondary School project and returned to his own country. 'The Father' had stood on the doorstep of her hut on the one night, with the light of the sun on his face. He had returned again the next night with the air of one who had come back to make a final statement about their past relationship. He had stood looking at her for a moment, with an intent expression, then he mentioned a name she could not later recall. At the same time he had flung back his head and laughed:

'Oh, the hells we two smashed up together!' he said.

'The Father', had had behind him, a gruesome woman, with no head. She was dressed in a long, black dress. The headless figure had slowly walked straight into Elizabeth. She underwent a transformation during the night, and at dawn she emerged from Elizabeth's chest area, in a burst of golden-yellow light. She had found her head again and was dressed in a soft, sun-yellow dress. She spread her arms out towards the rising sun and, with swimming movements of her bare feet, flew straight into its blazing depths. Elizabeth had thought about it for a while, puzzled, then it had passed away in the storm of the Sello-Medusa affair. The impression it had left behind, though, of 'the Father' was that he was a personality who had gone in for bloody and awful dramas. He remained a hero-image, to her.

Dan's words reinvoked him. She thought at first that Dan was a man who also admired the achievements of other men. She never thought of his evil subtleties, that he had said it deliberately, to create a hero-image of himself in her mind, to claim a greater achievement or status with her, without having to prove anything. There were many things she forgot at the time, especially the words of 'the Father'. He had said:

'Dan is fooling around with my name.'

Half of Medusa's words were true. Dan was dazzling enchantment. There was a feeling of fantastic magic in the air, like the words of an old love-song: 'You smile, the song begins. You speak and I hear violins. It's magic. . . .'

After all, didn't he know witless fools by now? He'd seen the reeling, collapsing performance of the Medusa triangle. He saw Sello, the monk, stripped of his vesture garments. Oh yes, the poor had told Sello to do so, and he, Dan, had a comment on the poor too. He said: 'I don't like them. They're so stupid and cruel.' Again, Elizabeth was taken off guard. Didn't she know some unpleasant details about tribal life, a basic cruelty and lack of compassion that was a part of the African personality? He suppressed a contempt for Sello. As for Elizabeth, he utterly despised her but it was a little too early to strip off the gloves. Elizabeth had real gold. She was loaded. He thrust it at her in a vivid picture. Her past lives and efforts appeared before her in the form of a billion small bags filled with gold. They glowed with a soft, yellow light. He moved his arms and gathered the bags to him.

'It was all perfection,' he said.

He looked at her. He was grinning widely. He raised a plain steel crown of a dull hue to his head. She looked straight and full into the grinning face. He was looking at a point beyond her, too, into the future. He was full of confidence. The African grin said so much. It was hatred. It was control of a situation. It was top-secret information: 'Pussy-cat, I'm da guy what knows what to do with all dat gold. I'm da keeper of all dat gold. Da philosopher types don't know what ta do wid dere gold. Huh, ya wanta see some flowers, liddle pussy? I know ya likes flowers an' pretty things.'

Elizabeth raised her hand, astonished. A beautiful pale pink blossom lay in it. It seemed to create the atmosphere for his next move (She was to find that Dan was a great one for the right atmosphere and lighting-effects). He grasped her firmly and sped away back along the path of the meteor. Its journey was flung far out, right to the outermost edge of the universe. There was a heaven there where the light had shaded down to a deep midnight blue. A man and a woman stood in it, wrapped in an eternal embrace. There were symbols of their love. There were two grape-trees with the roots entwined; there was a broad wide river coming down in full flood, with a tremendous roar, supposedly symbolic of a powerful, blind, all-consuming love. There was nothing else, no people, no sharing. It was shut-in and exclusive, a height of heights known only to the two eternal lovers. She awoke the next morning with the roar of that river in h.

ears. She was ill and broken down, unprepared in health for this new clamour. She crawled out of bed to set out some food for the small boy. There was some cake with pink sugar-icing and roast chicken. She set it down on the floor near his playthings. He would not bother her once he started on his inventions. She crawled back into bed.

It took a few minutes for the clamour in the air outside to reach her ears. There was a chorus of feminine voices singing: 'Glory be to God on high, on earth peace, goodwill towards men.'

She shook her head. It was impossible. She could not be hearing things too. She crawled out of bed, opened the door and walked out. There was not a soul in sight. It was Christmas Day. The chorus of singing was in the air, directly over her house. The unseen female choir repeated the words over and over: 'Glory be to God on high, on earth peace, goodwill towards men.'

Elizabeth listened, appalled. Nothing Sello had ever said in the beginning frightened her as much as this did. It implied that there was still something up there, unseen, unknown to account for. It was then she realized how deeply his earlier attitudes had influenced her thinking. He had introduced her to people. He had produced no phenomena. He had reproduced the solid beauty of life. He had said, in so many ways: 'God is people. There's nothing up there. It's all down here.'

Following the pattern of her learning, this was an abrupt contradiction of Sello's attitudes. These had seeped in somewhere so solidly into her own attitudes that she consciously thought of people as God-like, she worked out everything from that point. And yet since that early peaceful communication so much else had upheaved between her and Sello. What sort of gymnast was she supposed to be, so overstrained between concepts of good and evil? The insistent record was shattering. It went on and on. The first thing she thought of was that she had committed some terrible form of blasphemy against the unknown God by thinking people were he. The female chorus returned him to his absolute supremacy. She was intensely disturbed. It went on right through Christmas Day, any time she awoke in the night, and right through the following day, when it was abruptly switched off.

The air actually quivered with the question: 'Did ya get the message, pussy-cat? Who is God?'

She did not. The year of Medusa and her thunderbolts had brought her crashing down flat on her back. It took just this sort of phenomenon to knock her out completely. She lay in bed, sinking, sinking, uncaring about anything.

Kenosi came speeding down the small dusty brown road with the long, loping strides of a cat in haste. Her bent head nodded a little quicker than usual. It was two days after Christmas and the first day Elizabeth had stood up. The past two days had passed by for her in a slumbering delirium, but her shattered nerve-ends had knitted themselves together again. She had eaten nothing, though meals had been prepared. Almost ravenously she drank cup after cup of tea.

She had the door open by the time Kenosi reached the doorstep. Kenosi stared at her severely.

'Dumela,' she said, a little breathlessly. 'There is someone in the garden to join us in the work.'

'Who?' Elizabeth asked, instantly alert.

'I don't know him,' Kenosi said. 'He is saying he comes from America. His name is Tom. He's from farmer's side. One of the farmers told me he was sleeping in the dormitory with them. He came on Christmas Day.'

'Won't you come in for some tea first?' Elizabeth asked.

'There isn't time,' Kenosi said abruptly. 'The work must start.'

Elizabeth rushed to collect her garden notebook and bag. The small boy picked up his box of inventions and huffed and panted after them.

The gate-posts and corner-posts had to be fixed in with cement. He was already mixing the concrete for the gate-posts by the time they arrived in the garden. He was about twenty-two years old. He was stripped to the waist and wore faded blue jeans. From somewhere he had acquired a pair of army boots such as the cattlemen sometimes wear when they are taking their cattle on long treks through the bush. He looked up briefly as they approached. He had an absent-mindedly friendly face with slightly squinty blue eyes and a small mouth which he kept partly open. It made him look permanently surprised. His short-cropped hair stood straight on end. The two women paused. They were a perfect work-team together, silent, intent and yet always dependent on each other for a hand to lift a weight here and ease a load there. During the past week it had been fixed that they should work together. Here was a third party. He worked beautifully. He had hard, thick muscles on the arms and back and clutched the spade firmly with thick, grubby hands. He did not care about greetings. Maybe some other time. He was busy. Without looking up again he said to no one in particular:

'Will you catch hold of this pole, I'm just about to pitch in the cement.'

The gate-pole was in the hole at a slant. Kenosi stepped forward, grasped hold of it and clung to its upright posture. It was as if the young man's inner world was always one of ease and freedom, no matter what his circumstances. He started singing to himself:

'Hello, Dolly. This is Lewis, Dolly. It's so nice to have you back where you belong. You're looking swell, Dolly. I can tell, Dolly. You're still growing, you're still going, you're still going strong. ...'

Elizabeth listened to the words alertly. How they fitted her own circumstances! Maybe Dolly had been to hell and back.

'What happened to Dolly?' she interrupted. 'Why is Lewis greeting her like that? Was she in trouble of some kind?'

He kept silent a moment, then said: 'I don't know. I've forgotten the story. I saw the musical some time ago.'

He tapped the concrete smooth with the spade, whistling all the while that gay tune, then he swung the spade into the wheelbarrow. Suddenly he propelled himself around sharply from the hips and moved his heavy boots in an extraordinarily light tap dance, flinging his arms wide in the air: 'Gee, fellas, have a little faith in me, fellas,' he shrilled in a high off-key voice, 'Dolly ain't going away. Fellas, she'll never go away. Dolly ain't going away again. Yeeee-ow!'

Kenosi thoroughly enjoyed it. She raised a hand to her mouth to stifle a loud giggle. Elizabeth was ten years older than he. Suddenly she could place him. He looked exactly like the small boy who harassed her life with questions about goats falling off the edge of the earth. That was the surface, a rough, crude fellow, always dirty and smelling of sweat, so exhibitionistic that he seemed totally oblivious of persons. Where did any friendship begin of that other kind where people turn their heads slowly and stare deeply into the mystery of life? Because that was what she remembered most about him throughout that year – he kept on turning his head with a sudden deep expression of wisdom in his eyes. He said he'd just come out of university with a degree in agriculture. His job was to promote farmer's youth-development work-groups in other parts of the country such as the farm they had at the Motabeng Secondary School project. He had taken up lodgings with the farm students in their dormitory. He was supposed to leave in a few months' time for another village where a farm project was about to begin, but he looked around at the completely erected poles of the garden and said:

'I have time to start some work here.'

The dry stream-bed beside the garden kept a hidden memory of when water had flowed through it all the year round; a few immense shade trees grew close together at the bottom of the garden. The area seemed to whisper softly: 'Take me. Turn me into a one-acre plot of cabbage, green beans, carrots, beetroot, tomatoes, onions, peas and lettuce. You'd be surprised at all the fancy ladies with baskets on their arms who'll come and visit me. I have been so lonely with only goats to talk to. . . .'

She had the notes of the instant vegetable garden she had taken from Small-Boy. They were a combination of the deep trench bed and the transplanting of seedlings from plastic bags. Neither she nor Kenosi was capable of the heavy pick-digging work needed in the construction of the deep beds. Elizabeth handed him her notebook. He sat down on the ground and bent his head in deep concentration over it. Elizabeth nearly laughed out loud with relief when he took it all quite seriously. Her version of agriculture was so poetic

and fanciful, she was so liable to fill in her gaps of knowledge with self-invented agriculture, she so obviously amused
and irritated the English manager of the farm school that
here was a friend indeed. He said:

'I'll start digging out the beds for you once we've put in
the fence and gate-posts.'

'Has Gunner come back yet?' she asked eagerly.

'Yes,' he said. 'His wife invited me for supper last night.'

'They tell me Gunner designed the farm vegetable
garden,' she said. 'It has a big street down the middle with
lots of side streets between the beds. People can walk around
and look at everything. I think the vegetables like it too.
They like neatness and order.'

He screwed up his eyes as though slightly puzzled by this
information, but said nothing. It was past midday. There
were all the uneaten meals at her home. She mentioned this.
They all trailed up the pathway and down the dusty brown
road to her home, the small boy taking up the rear, his box
of inventions under his arm. The young man felt quite at
ease in other people's homes, as he did everywhere else. He
made straight for the kitchen sink and bathed himself from
head to waist. The water dripped down his arms on to the
floor in a small pool. Unconsciously he champed his big
boots around in the pool, widening the muddy area. Then he
swung into the small dining-room, hurled back a chair and
sat down on it with a loud thump. He placed two thick
hands firmly on the table and looked at the food with great
interest, and once he began eating he ate up everything in
sight, till not a crumb was left. There was a bowl of stew,
roast chicken, a bowl of rice, fruit puddings in jelly and a
cake with a small slice cut out of it.

'Any more of this delicious stew?' he said.

She picked up the bowl and went into the kitchen to
scrape the remnants of the stew out of the pot. As soon as
she set the bowl on the table, Tom picked it up and emptied
its entire contents on to his plate. She hadn't noticed the
small boy. He'd been set down in a corner on a mat with his
bowl. He barely ate two spoonfuls of rice and stew at lunch
and a spoonful of porridge in the morning. At some stage
he'd crept out of his corner and stood silently near Tom,

watching his appetite with open-mouthed fascination. He stretched out his bowl:

'Any more of this delicious stew?' he asked anxiously.

Without any interruption in his eating, Tom hurled a spoonful of the stew from his plate into the boy's bowl. The boy did not budge. He had to see how Tom put the food in his mouth. Here was something quite new. Just as Elizabeth put to one side her plate of half-eaten rice and stew, she was astonished to see it lifted high into the air and all its contents emptied on to Tom's plate.

Magic. Elizabeth was still living in the glow of that meteor-ride to the end of the universe, and the gentleman kept on sending the lady flowers. He could create whole fields of them, pretty innocent-looking wild flowers nestling in the kind of grass Adam and Eve must have seen in the garden of Eden. The grass and earth were luminous, and she was fanciful and poetic enough to be deeply impressed by these sights and distracted into thinking that she was faced with a creator of great beauty. As she watched these hazy visions of beauty, his soul came hurtling towards her with a big bang. That night things were going grrr, grrr, grrr, then click, to indicate all sorts of joining of their souls together. Hadn't she faced terrible hazards? Hadn't she been hit and hit with no defence or protection against super-natural thunderbolts?

'I'll protect you for ever, silly girl,' he said.

He gave the impression of power to match his words.

In this soul-to-soul contact Dan also said, quite abruptly: 'I don't care what I do.'

The woman was incredibly stupid, so impressionable that her mind could take great leaps into wild dangers without perceiving them as such. She immediately thought: 'Ah, I'm just the same. I don't care what I do, for a cause, for some-one I love, for my convictions.' She never paused and sorted out the wide gap between the man's statement and her own personality pattern. She linked his words up to a hero-image he had subtly built on another man's efforts. The other man was not a reality. He was a soul-personality, far removed, untouchable. Dan was alive in Motabeng village.

Next he said: 'You nearly died over the past two days. I was holding your soul back. I am much bigger than you. My soul is too powerful.'

In a twinkling, a woman shot into the room, later to be known as B......, The Womb. She was a local woman. She wore a black silk dress. It clung tightly to her heavily-built body. She bent over at an angle and raised one thick, firm leg halfway in the air, like a ballerina. Her face glowed with the same light that lit up the flowers nestling in the grass of the garden of Eden. She stood unshakeably on one leg. She had a broad, firm back. The implications cried loudly: 'You can't do that. Why, you'd wobble like hell and topple over.' So it was all right for him to say:

'She'll serve as the balance between us.'

No further explanations were given of what was really a puzzling statement. What did it really mean? What balance, and how did this balance work out? It was left like that. The woman was simply left balancing on one leg like a ballerina, and certainly Elizabeth was highly collapsible material. Anything toppled her over, a thunderbolt, a command, any suggestion of powerful assertiveness.

He was in such a hurry. He had so much to accomplish that he threw scene after scene at her. He next had himself standing next to a man. Dan was clothed in a soft, white cloth, resembling the one Sello wore. He had on a pair of sandals. The man next to him was haranguing a crowd. The veins in his forehead and throat bulged, he splayed his hands out in the air, he talked with great intensity, he wanted to impress people, to dominate. By contrast, Dan bent humbly down, he folded his hands softly in front of him, his face wore a sad, still expression: 'You see,' it said. 'That's the essence of me. In my soul I am the monk. I can never err like that man. I can never dominate.'

In the quietness, a small white card was pushed in front of her gaze. It said simply: 'Directorship since 1910.'

She sat up alertly in the dark. She was beginning to get the message. It was put over powerfully, with a chorus of angels' voices in the air. It was put over humbly. It was put over beautifully in the garden of Eden. It was put over with a card. Her head must be pretty dim. Why, that must be

God. He certainly had the power and force to back up his claims, a sort of spinning, revolving, eternal motion, a sort of power behind all powers that kept everything in its place, that kept the stars up there, in fact the feel of everything that made the universe revolve around the universe. Ought a person not to turn over and sleep peacefully? Everything would be taken care of. The nightmare of the past year was over.

Torture. Something had gone wrong between sleeping and waking. She stepped out of bed and skidded on slime. She held out two shaky, unsteady hands and turned her head from side to side in anguish. Wave after wave of obscenity was beating against her head. Oh, there had been a release from it for a week or so after Medusa's ending. She had felt back in her own form again, back in her own house. She turned to run. Hell was there in full force again. It was peculiar this time. The person wasn't asserting evil. He was saying he had the potential to be evil, and he was saying awful things about molesting children. He couldn't be trusted to be alone with children or else he'd do awful things to them. And he was saying awful things about Dan. Dan was a child-molester too, but much worse still, he went for other men like mad. Once the record was turned on in her head it just went on and on in the same groove. It was so powerful and insistent that it had the effect of killing the beauty of the living world and trapping her inside its clamour. Her whole nervous system shook under the strain. Painfully, she looked out on the new day. The sun had started its curving pathway across the blue, drought-stricken sky. A small bird in a tree outside her house cockily puffed up his tiny chest and burst into a loud, trilling song.

'People aren't like that,' she countered, helplessly, muttering aloud to herself. 'They get up and work. They lose their thoughts in inventing things and battling with the problems of life. It's not like this, a ruthless concentration on the obscene.'

It did not help. The record churned on monotonously the whole day, and the day passed in a blur of pain. She was helping Kenosi and Tom to attach the fence-wire to the poles in the garden. It wasn't that it was unfamiliar to her.

It was the nightmare of the slums she had grown up in in South Africa, but it never dominated life. Usually small girls got raped, but the men were known. 'The law' caught up with them. Homosexuals were laughingly accepted as one of the oddities of life, but they never unduly disturbed people. Perhaps totally normal people don't think about it at all because it isn't their problem. What was she to do with this record inside her head? It was more real because it had feeling behind it too, a cringing, deep shame. As she crawled miserably into bed that night, the culprit was exposed. It was 'the Father'. He was standing in an open space and confessing his evil. The roots of it were uncovered. She suffered too, because he had attached to her a long thread-like filament like an umbilical cord. It was pitch-black in colour, supposedly signifying evil or darkness. As he confessed in agony, this dark thread separated. An outraged Dan stood near him. He said, indignantly: 'He said he was the King of the Underworld, didn't he? Then that's where he's going.' Dan uncurled a long rope and flung it in lasso formation over 'the Father's' neck.

'Come on, go to hell!' Dan shouted and dragged him away.

She made a comparison between the two scenes. The man who had declared to her that he was the King of the Underworld had said it with the triumph of one who had brought all evil under his control. She looked at the present scene almost indifferently. The personality of 'the Father' was ice and rigid self-control. An explanation soon emerged. Dan approached her and said, brokenly: 'He does that to me because he loves you too. There are so many people against us.'

When he talked of love to her there was a pathetic appeal in his tone. His love was exclusive, between her and him alone. They ought to be silently wrapped up in it, with no intruders. The pathetic appeal had a corresponding appeal in her. He'd flung a hook right into her pain- and feeling-centre. This he was to use as he pleased: 'Now cry, now laugh, now feel jealous.' And he adjusted the button to suit his needs.

She could understand, too, his jealousy of 'the Father'.

There wasn't any soul as spectacular or as dashing as he. He'd been cast from the start in the mould of a superman. He raised his majestic head and surveyed the universe with cold eyes and supreme indifference. He was a multi-billion-aire who had never cared to examine his estate, because alongside his estate he'd been handed beggars' rags. Even these he wore with the stately bearing of a king in fine raiment. A comic side drama was to be played all through-out that year between Dan and 'the Father'. Like Sello, in his white cloth, 'the Father' had silently taken up a position in her house. It was just near the top of her bed, near the left side. She could see Sello, but she could not see 'the Father', and had been totally unaware of his presence until it became a mania to Dan. A few nights after he had dragged 'the Father' to hell, Dan stood staring at the top end of her bed. Suddenly he flung his arm high into the air and said in a voice of loud command: 'Go!'

The person would not budge. Dan stretched out a hand and hauled him into view. 'The Father' passively allowed himself to be shoved out of the house. A short while later he was back again. 'The Father' was frantically pushed over cliffs, sent hurtling to his death in a wildly out-of-control motor car, but he had nine thousand soul-lives. He always turned up again. He made no counter-attack on Dan. He passively offered himself for each death, only to soar back into life again. One night 'the Father' quietly approached Elizabeth. His manner was of one who did not want to be overheard. He stared with wide, blue eyes at a distant horizon and said softly, dispassionately:

'He's going to blow you up so hard, there won't be any-thing left of you. Try and protect yourself in some way.' And instantly he vanished.

What was going on? He had indicated that he was not on call for help. It was a road so lonely, so isolated in suffering that when her endurance snapped, she became totally in-coherent. There was a whole range of silent observers. They were passive. One or two bolted out of hidden obscurity towards her at moments of peak suffering with frightened whispers: 'We want to see everything. He does not want the new world.'

It was a deliberate trap and counter-trap, with her soul thrown right into the firing-line. It was David and Goliath all over again, only this time David had no sling, was helplessly feminine and faced a monster no one could imagine in their wildest dreams. Apparently, he appeared so isolated too on their lonely battlefield because the forces of hell had sent up 'the brains'. It took her ages to work out Dan's subtleties, if she ever did at the time. Innocent-looking words, gestures, expressions of people were turned against them by him into the perverse, the obscene, till there was nothing that was not tainted with perversity.

To show how deeply he had been involved all along in Sello's activities, Dan re-paraded the beautiful people in front of her, but this time as chain-gang slaves. They had the sheepish expressions of people with hidden evils; he hauled one or two of them out of the crowd and exposed their hidden potential for crime. He did this vigorously, with authority, so that their potential for evil seemed an absolute certainty. There was a man who was the keeper of all the joys of family life. He was shown sitting in a car till dawn, in the embrace of a prostitute. His wife committed suicide. All the men were like that, they had prostitutes in the background. A long story was to unfold about the women. Half of them belonged to Dan.

Who was there to offer a word in their defence? No one defended them. The beautiful people were Sello's original vision, and his comment at that time had been: 'Some of them are perfect already.' He let them alone. When he said anything about evil at all, it was about his own self and the woman he had loved. And he had said: 'I am the root cause of human suffering.' Now he just sat there in his scarecrow's rags, indifferent to everything. Hadn't Dan waited for this hour? Where did the prophecies come in now? Sello had damned himself. It was all over with Sello. The last blow to the prophecies was 'da pussy-cat'. A thousand things Elizabeth sensed, the jarring jazzy undertone of a razzle-dazzle show, the sense of being thought of as a helpless pet 'silly girl', 'darling', while in reality, all her life, she was the sort of woman men never said foolish, tender things to. Men just didn't get that close, and she had really decided to marry because she was getting old, and tired of sitting in libraries with books.

Next to 'the Father' the half-mad Asian man with the ferocious eyes had made the most impact on her mind. He had only cared about the poor. He had appeared to dislike Elizabeth for an inability, apparently in past destinies, to make a floor-crawling identity with the truly humble and lowly. Here everything was to be set right. Africa was to teach her how, so he said. He was pounced on by Dan and pulled to the forefront and made to confess his crime. His brilliant, glittering black eyes were changed to an imbecilic docility. He had on a white shirt; the sleeves were torn; four grinning, smirking Asian men clung to his arms. He was a homosexual.

That took care of the lot of them. He did not have to say it, it had already been vividly stated in pictures and imagery; all was evil. Then he turned to his Herculean task, the death of Sello. A coffin was carried into her room. In it was the Sello of the brown suit with his narrow, mean eyes. Six people carried the coffin. Four of them were women who kept their faces turned away from Elizabeth. In the centre was Dan. He had his handsome face screwed up with torture, but screwed so prettily it still looked handsome. Someone else turned her face towards Elizabeth. It was a little girl who was one of Sello's children. Elizabeth recognized her because she often rode beside him in his green truck through Motabeng village.

The heavy boots twinkled to a stop outside her gate. He looked up expectantly and shouted: 'Here I am!'

Tom always did that so that the door would open and he could fly straight into the house. He never really seemed to walk, he was so light on his feet that his boots barely touched the ground, and he was always in a tremendous hurry. He'd not been two weeks in Motabeng before his reputation for hard work and giving a hand anywhere had spread like wildfire. There were so many jobs for him, he flew around everywhere. The village women saw him working with Kenosi and Elizabeth in the garden, and one morning, as Elizabeth was walking with him down to the garden, a group of women was high up on the rafters busy thatching a hut.

'Tom! Tom!' they called, already knowing his name. 'Come here and help us.'

He stopped abruptly and looked up at the laughing women, then he turned eagerly towards Elizabeth and said: 'Hell, I'd like to learn that job. I don't know how to thatch.'

He shouted back at the women: 'I'm coming.'

He did everything on sudden, wild impulses like that. A few days after he had arrived in Botswana, he had confided to Elizabeth that he loved the country and had decided to take out citizenship.

'What about your mother in America?' Elizabeth had asked. 'She'll miss you.'

He was highly offended.

'I don't need mothers,' he had said abruptly.

He sailed into the house, beaming. He put a parcel on the draining-board of the sink, stripped off a soiled orange shirt and flung it over the board. There was a big hole at the back of his orange shirt, and as he washed his face and arms in the sink the water ran down his arms into a pool on the floor. He moved his boots in the pool, creating a huge area of muddy water. Elizabeth kept her house scrupulously polished up and clean, and yet she liked it.

'Elizabeth,' he said busily. 'I've brought a loaf of bread so I don't eat all your food. Did you make that delicious stew as you promised?'

'Where's your nose?' Elizabeth asked, smiling. The odour of the herbs and spices in the stew filled the whole house.

People made unlikely friendships on the Motabeng projects. First they were thrown together through work. Then, everyone talked English of some kind. Then it seemed that people from other parts of the world were very similar to people in Africa, but she wasn't the sort of person Tom could get along with. In every way he showed that he liked lots of company and was as carelessly gregarious as his walk. People were a blur he grasped together with wide open arms, indiscriminately. They were all friends. At the end of their lives they'd both have the same number of friends, but Elizabeth's would be known and known deeply. Tom's would be unknown to him. She could see it in his gestures. He moved about restlessly, shifted and twisted distractedly, but when a face or word arrested his attention, he caught hold of himself and sat and stared like a quiet, still spider trapped in a corner, looking at life with gently-waving feelers. It must have been the second time he came to eat at her house that she noticed that he was not only rough, carefree, crude. He had the most beautiful expression of deep wisdom in his eyes, and turned and stared at her like an ancient man.

They were talking about James Baldwin and other writers they loved. Soon she stopped taking note of what she was saying, because afterwards she could not remember a word of the conversation, except the feeling it had left behind: 'Why,' she thought, 'I've seen him somewhere before, and I'll keep on seeing him again and again in the future. I'll keep on meeting him.' It was the vastness and freedom of it, a friendliness towards another which was always tentative and yet secure. He liked to bang into her and say:

'Elizabeth, I'm cooking supper for a whole lot of people. Come along.'

And she'd shrink: 'I can't do that, Tom. I like to talk to you alone.'

He'd keep quiet a moment, then say: 'Allright, when I'm not busy I'll come and eat at your house.'

That whole day, work had moved on a high tide. The local-industries project had suddenly burst out into a hive of activity. She stood by the sink and laughed:

'You know, Tom,' she said. 'You'd never believe Eugene was like a child. He came back and found the garden completely fenced. He depends on that kind of encouragement, because he suddenly decided to get all the local-industry buildings completed too. You know Kenosi? There's no one like her for making a speech about working with her hands. He took Kenosi along to a meeting with the builders of the youth-development work-group and asked her to make a speech. The students were overcome. They said to Kenosi: "If local industries can help people, then we can help local industries." They agreed to work and erect the buildings for no bonus. I know what that means, because they built my house and had meeting after meeting demanding the bonus.

Eugene must be saying: "Why didn't I think about it before?", because no one likes the project. It's too tough.'

He was wiping his face. He paused and looked over the bath towel.

'Eugene,' he said intensely. 'I love him so much! As for Kenosi, there's no other woman like her on earth. She's special.'

Tom had also brought Gunner down to the garden. Gunner had divided up the garden into Main Street, or Broadway, with about forty side-streets between the long narrow beds. Gunner was so shy that he never looked directly at anyone, but he kept a permanent smile in his eyes. He had a reddish complexion. When he spoke, his style was that of the common market-vendor, or like the humility and humanity of the slum men Elizabeth had grown up amongst. He said to Elizabeth: 'We must do our best to help others, mustn't we?' Black men of the slums talked like that. No wonder Small-Boy had chosen him as his ideal and imitated his method of careful and methodical present-ation of information. She seemed to hear Small-Boy talking again as Gunner turned to her at one point and said:

'When you practise crop-rotation there is a formula to follow; legumes such as beans and peas follow a leaf-crop like cabbage, lettuce or spinach, followed by a root-crop such as beetroot, carrots or turnip. After this you may try a rotation of a second root-crop such as tomatoes, potatoes or onions. Then start again with your legumes.'

Elizabeth had also carefully dried and preserved the seeds of Thoko's big yellow pumpkin. There were lots of exca-vation-like holes in the garden, made when the knotted roots of the thorn-bush had been dug out. In these holes she planted the pumpkin seed. The drought weather usually broke at this time of the year, late summer, and already deep mists in the early morning were heralds of rain. But a bore-hole for underground water had been drilled for the local-industries project, and since the gardeners were racing ahead with their work, Eugene had spent the whole day digging a trench that would bring a water-pipe into the garden. There was a tremendous clashing and banging of work-tools all around as the students swarmed over the construction-works

in their green overalls. Villagers passed by and stared at it all
with mute, enquiring faces. There were always a few village
people who would step forward for voluntary work. About
forty had joined the project. Most of them were working in
the houses of the teachers of Motabeng Secondary School
making soap, mats, blankets, pots, plates, cups, teapots,
dresses and any other item that could be invented for the
shop's opening day. The rest of the villagers wanted to wait
and see. They were not mad enough to start working for no
money; poor people liked money.

Tom had started digging out the trench-beds of the garden.
They had to be dug down to a depth of two feet and then
refilled with a blending of manure, soil and fertiliser. Kenosi
and Elizabeth worked behind his pick, quickly scooping out
the loosened earth with spades, but in the midday heat they
sat under the shade-trees at the bottom of the garden and
prepared seedlings in plastic bags for transplanting into the
trench-beds as soon as they were ready. Into each small
plastic bag with its six inches of soil-manure mixture they
dropped four cabbage seeds. Eventually, after a month, and
with gradual thinning, each bag would hold one gigantic
cabbage seedling. They'd make holes with spades in the
trench-beds, then cut away the plastic and place each seedling with its mould of earth into the holes. Almost overnight
a gardener had his instant vegetable garden. Not one seedling died during transplanting. Cabbages, tomatoes, cauliflower and peppers appeared as if from nowhere and grew
with shimmering, green leaves in the intense heat. They were
making the half-rotting orders of green vegetables from
Johannesburg a thing of the past. Somewhere at the back
of her mind, Elizabeth was bewildered by events. Kenosi, the
fear of another mental breakdown, the sudden appearance of
Tom, had thrust her into a clamour of work. But how that
year of 1970 was to reel and reel right to the depths of
hell!

The small boy quietly opened the door and crept into the
house. His face was radiant. The holidays were lonely because some of his playtime friends went with their mothers
to the lands to plough, and some, like Jimmy, went to the
fishing and game reserves in Northern Botswana with their

parents. Tom swung around and caught hold of him just as he was about to go and hide in a córner.

'Hello, Shorty,' he said. 'And what did you learn at school today?'

The small boy was called Shorty because he refused to grow. He seemed to remain the height he was when he was three years old. He had just started the beginners' grade at school.

'I learned about evaporation,' he said to Tom, with a shy dignity.

'And what can you tell me about it?' asked Tom.

The small boy quivered eagerly into life.

'I drawed it,' he said.

With great excitement, he dived under his couch bed for his small school suitcase, fumbled in it and handed Tom a notebook. Tom studied it for a moment, then said:

'Hey, wait a bit. You've spelt evaporation wrong. It's evaporation not ivaporation.'

The small boy looked at him, stunned.

'It's right,' he said, indignantly. 'I copied it from the board like that. My teacher spells it like that.'

Tom shook his head: 'You must have made a mistake, Shorty. It's wrong.'

'It's right,' insisted the small demon. 'My teacher spells it like that.'

'Elizabeth,' Tom called loudly. 'Where's your dictionary?'

Elizabeth pointed to a shelf of books in her bedroom. Tom jumped up energetically, muttering: 'Phew! I've never seen such a stubborn child in my life before.'

Elizabeth was setting the supper food on the table. They argued vehemently. In the end Tom had to give up. The small boy's teacher won. Incredulously Tom approached her the following day. He said he'd shot around to the primary school section of Motabeng Secondary School. The small boy's teacher was a young Motswana girl, just out of training college. He'd peeped into the small boy's classroom. Sure enough, evaporation was spelt wrong, so were all the other English words.

'She's a hell of a pretty girl,' he said. 'But she can't spell. There's something right somewhere though. It's absolutely correct spelling if it's phonetics. It's phonetics she's using.'

Elizabeth laughed: 'It's all right, Tom,' she said. 'Wherever English travels, it's adapted. That's Setswana English. Setswana is an entirely phonetic language.'

Who would knowingly take a journey into hell? At the end of it Sello said something like: 'You are just the same.' It was as if he was muttering hopefully under his breath. He wanted to include Elizabeth in too many of his crimes and prophecies. His relationship with Medusa had appeared as a form of retribution for his sins, but even then Elizabeth had woven out her own romantic dreams about his Madonna: 'He's saying goodbye, for ever, and he's saying it brutally.' In their heyday together as Medusa and Caligula, Medusa had obviously flattered him to the teeth. She did not like a person to even think that Sello might look like a monkey.

There was nothing beautiful in the Dan story. He was the 'big-time' guy from hell. They must have had a conference down there. It must have gone something like this:

'Say, Dan, who's spoiling da party all da time?'

Dan, smiling: 'It's da Buddha.'

'You tink dat guy got brains like you, Dan? We can surely moider dat bum, put his feet in cement and dump 'im at da bottom of da Indian Ocean.'

Dan, smiling: 'Here's da plan.'

Dan had been holding on to his thing for, it must have been, two weeks. He did not want to upset Elizabeth and the phenomena of heaven he'd staged for her. Besides, he had to fix up his electrical wiring system (her whole body was a network, a complicated communication centre); everything depended on the efficiency of it. He couldn't get the wires in the right place if she was nervy or jumpy. As soon as the stage was set, he let loose. This was his version of God.

That night he was jumping up and down like mad.

'My whole body is on fire,' he said, then he looked at Elizabeth accusingly and added: 'It's you. You are not supposed to think of me with any desire, or else I shall fall down.'

He did not specify from what height.

The next night he introduced a girl. She had her hair done

up in the traditional style; small chunks of hair were tied on to a length of string and wound round and round the head. The girl bowed her head so that Elizabeth could get a good look at her hair-do. Dan said:

'I like girls like this with that kind of hair. Your hair is not properly African.'

She wasn't the usual sort of girl. She was a specialist in sex. A symbol went hand in hand with her, a small sewing-machine with a handle.

'She can go with a man the whole night and feel no ill-effects the next day, provided you stimulate her properly,' Dan explained.

The stimulation worked like a sewing-machine; turn the handle with a big swing, then the needle rattles up and down; turn the handle again and so on. It looked as if the key to it was her penny-button. She liked her penny-button tickled.

His other comment on Miss Sewing-Machine was: 'She's a demon of self-control.'

Then he simply tumbled the girl into bed beside Elizabeth and went with her the whole night. The lights on the cinema screen of her mind were down, but not their activity. They kept on bumping her awake till at dawn they made the last bump, bump, bump.

He pressed several buttons at the same time:

You are supposed to feel jealous.

You are inferior as a Coloured.

You haven't got what that girl has got.

The records went round and round in her head the whole day. He turned on a record of whatever happened to be the issue of the moment. The poor man had been sent into the job with a leprosy-like fear of Coloureds or half-breeds. That was one of his favourite records. He was afraid he might have to touch the half-breed at some time and contaminate his pure black skin, because he turned these records on so violently that they reached pitches of high, screaming hysteria in her mind. At one time she paused and puzzled it out. It strangely resembled the first record she had heard: 'Dog, filth, the Africans will eat you to death.' As soon as he noticed she was catching on to something, he made a bold admission: 'It was I. I did it. You were so loyal to that fool Sello in spite of what they were doing to you.'

And what about the new records? Oh, that was supposed to be his sense of humour.

'I'm a big tease,' he said.

But he thrust black hands in front of her, black legs and a huge, towering black penis. The penis was always erected. From that night he kept his pants down; after all, the women of his harem totalled seventy-one. They were a motley crew, half of them presented as goddesses with slight defects and the others as local girls. The local girls were supposed to benefit enormously from contact with his soul. They were supposed to be filled with power and sweet things they lacked and they were fillers for the time when his professionals were resting.

Miss Sewing-Machine belonged to the goddess class. Apparently she had been Dan's wife or soul-partner for one thousand past incarnations. Her considerable sexual ability, though, had also made her desire other men, and this Dan could not stand. For the purposes of the future, which he said was going to be perfect, she had to be cleaned up a little. He told her to go and wash in Elizabeth's bath-tub. Apparently, this would stop her promiscuity. In every way Dan could not conceal his contempt for Elizabeth, but strangely this contempt did not reach to her personal possessions. They seemed to have the property of cleaning up 'dirt'. He was abnormally obsessed with dirt on his women. They washed and washed in her bathroom; they put on Elizabeth's dresses and underwear and made use of her perfumes. The poor things had it drilled into them; any possession of Elizabeth's they could get hold of would give them some kind of holy immunity or make them doubly attractive. They stole with reckless speed, anything they could lay their hands on. Some of the women were taken from that early vision of the beautiful people. These were treated with holy awe; he was more fanatically attached to them than they to him, but they were still his slaves. It was the 'nice-time girls', he moaned to Elizabeth, who had plagued his destiny.

Whatever she was, Miss Sewing-Machine topped the lot of

them. Elizabeth was to remember her with deep affection. She was the only part of the nightmare that could express normal, human feelings; she was alternately sad, wistful, kind, and lonely, and when she laughed she laughed like the wind rushing through the trees. She always looked at Elizabeth as though she knew what friendships between women were really like, and she stood out like a star of beauty in a howling inferno.

The next night he had a new girl – Miss Wriggly-Bottom. She looked Chinese; she was quite yellow, and her long, straight, black hair cascaded over her bare shoulders. The girl didn't care for clothes; she was stark naked. Miss Sewing-Machine had a dress on till the lights dimmed. Wriggly-Bottom had small round breasts and a neat, nipped-in waist. She walked in time to a silent jazz tune she was humming and wriggled and wriggled her bottom. Then she lay herself down on the bed, on her tum, and propped her chin up in her hands. She looked at Elizabeth with enchanting black eyes.

'I'm just waiting for my date,' she said.

The date dimmed the lights.

He seemed to think this was getting a bit too much, even for the Coloured dog, Elizabeth, because the next morning he turned on a softer record. It said:

'My darling, if you call me I'll come to you. I don't like women like that, they're too cheap.'

Apparently he liked the girls to keep their clothes on until he told them to take them off. Then that night he had a dramatic announcement to make. Miss Wriggly-Bottom was stone dead. He'd overestimated her stamina. She couldn't go with a man the whole night. Her sex was outside, on her bust and thighs, it wasn't inside. There was just a vacuum inside. Then he said:

'I have an insatiable desire,' and in he hauled Miss Sewing-Machine again. She was looking desperately sad and wistful, but she temporarily solved his problem. The next day he was free to turn his attention back to his job, which was, of course, directing the affairs of the universe. The universe couldn't be set right until Sello was either set right, or dead.

He turned on the obscene record again:

'They all know what he's really after. It's got nothing to do with the prophecies. It's just sex. They all know him. They all know what he's like.'

The whole day long the record went on and on. She had tended to forget Sello in this sudden explosion of drama, and the silent, immobile figure on the chair said nothing at all. There had always been comments of some kind, even if it was a comment on an everyday event. What was resurrected before her gaze that night was the Sello in the brown suit, with his narrow, mean eyes. She had just started to doze fitfully – for three nights the 'goings-on' on her bed had kept her awake – when suddenly a cold slime touched her mouth. She looked up into the foxy face of Sello and raised one hand to brush the slime off her mouth. He caught hold of her hands in a vice-grip; he was grinning awfully. Half choking with fear, she struggled violently to free her hands and awoke with a piercing scream.

From his room the small boy began to whimper. She sprang out of bed and lit a candle.

'What's wrong?' he asked as she approached him. He was trembling.

'Don't bogey-men frighten you?' she asked. 'I saw an awful one just now.'

He stared at her with wide round eyes.

'What did he look like?' he asked. 'Will I see him too?'

Her nerves were snapping between the strain of the nightmares and the strain of the records during the day. Illogically she said to the child:

'I'll get some tablets in the morning.'

'What's that?' he asked.

'It's tablets for sleeping,' she said. 'The tablets make you sleep.'

'Can I have tablets too?'

'Only if you see horrid things when you sleep,' she said.

'Oh, no, I don't,' he said, relieved. 'I saw Father Christmas. You know, when Father Christmas wants to give you a present he just pushes it to you. Then I eat biscuits with cream. I always open the biscuit quickly and lick the cream. . . .'

He sat bolt upright in bed. His wonderland at night was too exciting. He went on and on; there were rabbits, playtime friends, dogs, chocolates -- the list was endless. At the end of it he said: 'I must make a present for Father Christmas in the morning, because he gives me a lot of things.'

He lay back and instantly fell asleep. She remained seated by his bed staring into the black night. There was a deep wail of tears inside her, as yet unexpressed.

'Oh God, help me,' she whispered.

She wasn't thinking coherently at all, or sorting anything out. She was just the receiver of horror, her whole life was suspended. She was losing track of the personality pattern she'd lived with since birth. It was being thrust aside by one monstrous event after another. Did it help if one sat silently in the night and cried? Did it help if the insects in the garden broodingly talked to themselves? Did it help, if on and off one had been kind and tender and humorous and could not comprehend permanent brutal savagery? No, it did not. She crawled into bed and began to doze fitfully. A gun swept into the air right before her gaze. An invisible hand was making the trigger go click, click, click. The gun glowed vividly in front of her, bathed in a yellow light. Dan said: 'He's not going to die in five years' time. He's going to die this year.'

She opened her eyes. It was dawn. She seemed to be lying in a pool of icy water. She was bathed from head to toe in a cold sweat.

Tom half raised the fork to his mouth, then put it down and pushed his full plate of food away from him. So surprising was this gesture that Elizabeth also put down her fork and stared at him, amazed. Nothing ever seemed to bother his appetite.

'I'm fed up,' he said.

He looked at her with wide, hurt eyes.

'Didn't you hear the news?' he said. 'My country has invaded Cambodia.'

Elizabeth kept quiet. She followed the world news over BBC world service each morning in a dazed fashion; a military coup in Africa, the Middle East crisis, a busmen's strike in London – it just went on and on. That he took Cambodia so personally discomforted her. She'd hardly heard or grasped the implications.

'I don't know why they bother to involve themselves in world affairs,' he continued. 'Wherever America goes she only hands the poor Coca-Cola and chewing-gum. They don't care a hell about rapid economic development.'

Rapid economic development was his pet subject. He'd earnestly tried to impress upon Elizabeth that she ought to support, morally, Mao Tse-tung, Castro and Nyerere because they stood for rapid economic development. He'd included Nkrumah, who had already disappeared in a coup. When Elizabeth protested he said, quite calmly: 'Nkrumah made a few errors, that's all. But he stood for rapid economic development.'

Now he turned to Elizabeth and said: 'The only people in my country who support rapid economic development are the Black Power people. . . .'

Suddenly he sprang to his feet, thrust one fist high into the air and said: 'Black Power!'

She looked up at him, alarmed: 'Do black people really do that? Do they really go around sticking their fists in the air like that?'

He looked down at her surprised: 'Of course,' he said. 'That's the slogan.'

'I don't like it,' she said, angrily. 'It only needs a Hitler to cause an explosion.'

'What!' he shouted. 'Are you mad? People are demanding their rights. I admire them.'

'What the bloody hell was Hitler doing? He also stuck his fist in the air,' she said, near to tears.

He sat down and looked at her earnestly: 'It's not the same thing,' he said. 'They're right. You don't know America.'

'I don't like exclusive brotherhoods for black people only. They wouldn't want you. You're not black.'

'I don't care a damn,' he said.

Somewhere at the back of her mind the conversation sounded extremely foolish. He was treating politics the way he treated people, a blur he embraced vaguely. He was a stupid person to argue with, if innate generosity of heart could be called stupid. He had the same idea about her.

'Just what's wrong with you?' he asked. 'Why do you have to go opposite to everyone else? Why do you have to sound different?'

'I've got my concentration elsewhere,' she said. 'It's on mankind in general, and black people fit in there, not as special freaks and oddities outside the scheme of things, with labels like Black Power or any other rubbish of that kind.'

He bent his head and started eating.

'Tom,' she said earnestly, 'once you make yourself a freak and special any bastard starts to use you. That's half of the fierce fight in Africa. The politicians first jump on the bandwagon of past suffering. They're African nationalists and sweep the crowd away by weeping and wailing about the past. Then why do they steal and cheat people once they get into government? They don't view the African masses as having any dignity or grandeur. They're just illiterates who don't know anything, so they think they can get up there and steal and cheat and squander the money. Every time there's a coup someone's been stealing and cheating. Then someone else steals and there's another coup. They don't ever see that the roots of it lie in their despising of the illiterate masses.'

He nodded his head: 'You're right about Africa,' he said. 'But you're wrong about America. People are literate there and they know what they're doing. They're doing the right thing.'

'It seems an indignity to me to stick a fist in the air,' she said quietly. 'I couldn't do it. I'd feel ashamed.'

'Why?'

'Because of what I see inside,' she said. 'Because of what I'm learning, internally.'

She hesitated, floundering. Did one make speeches right inside hell? Any heaven, like a Black-Power heaven, that existed for a few individuals alone was pointless and useless. It was an urge to throttle everyone else to death. Didn't she know about it in Southern Africa? Wasn't she a part of it in feeling when there was so much despair and so little hope? There had been statements by the South African government. They said they had enough weapons of war to blast the African continent into oblivion in half an hour. That being so, they rested in their evil, even boldly propagated it by increasing repressive laws. What was she learning here in the heaving turmoil of her inner life? She stood up quietly.

'There's some such thing as black people's suffering being a summary of everything the philosophers and prophets ever said,' she said. 'They said: "Never think along lines of I and mine. It is death." But they said it prettily, under the shade of Bodhi trees. It made no impact on mankind in general. It was for an exclusive circle of followers. Black people learnt that lesson brutally because they were the living victims of the greed inspired by I and mine and to hell with you, dog. Where do you think their souls are, then, after centuries of suffering? They're ahead of Buddha and Jesus and can dictate the terms for the future, not for any exclusive circle but for mankind in general.'

Elizabeth paused. She was a great orator. She had her audience of one captivated. The small boy had learned to ignore the high drama of the household. He went on eating.

'Tom,' she said softly. 'If you saw the soul of the black man the way I saw it, you'd feel afraid. Pretty mental analysis is nothing compared to the real thing. I saw it like this.'

She turned her head to one side and assumed the deeply scarred expression of the poor who had addressed her some time ago. She raised one hand and drooped it softly.

'That's what Buddha said,' she said. 'Avoid the greed in the heart. They had the whole message in their posture, in the softly drooping hand. It was a hand that did not want power of any kind because power and ambition had never been a part of their world. They said to me: "We are a people who have suffered", and they showed me their bare feet which were cut and bleeding from having been hounded for so long from all sides. We looked at each other silently. In the exchange of looks they said: "Are you truthful? Because we are. We know evil deeply and we know how to end it. We know its roots. We know its creators. They're nothing like the white fools shoving us around. They aren't the source of it, the powerful factory where it's actually manufactured. But you know. What about the arrogance of the soul, its wild flaring power, its overwhelming lust for dominance and prestige? Don't you know all that, the spring, then the river, then the ocean of horror?" I was stunned, Tom. Ever since that day I looked at things quite differently: Africa isn't rising. It's up already. It depends on where one places the stress. I place it on the soul. If it's basically right there, then other things fall into place. That's my struggle, and that's black power, but it's a power that belongs to all of mankind and in which all mankind can share.'

He had a way of sailing straight up to heaven when anything touched his heart. He turned towards her a face flaming with light. He said under his breath: 'Oh, oh, oh. That's right. Yes, that's right.'

She looked back at him with tortured eyes. She was talking uphill against a terrible downward pull. There was hell and hell and she was so broken down she couldn't last out for very long. The records of obscenity shook her nervous system from end to end. It was like the shock waves of an electrical current with a hand at the other and pressed firmly on the button.

'Tom,' she said. 'There comes a time when a sense of goodness awakens in one. I was not aware of it until . . .'

Before she could complete her sentence, he swung around on her, his eyes wide with surprise.

'The same thing happened to me a few years ago,' he burst out. 'It was so compelling that I decided to become a priest. I went and talked it over with a man who was greater than I and he said to me: "Tom, take that feeling into life among people. It serves no good purpose in a monastery. You test its strength in the battlefield." A few days later I thought: "What do billions of people in the world need? Food." That's why I went into agriculture. . . .'

He bent his head a moment, then shook it slowly.

'I sometimes suffer so much,' he said. 'I do things of which I am later bitterly ashamed.'

She looked at his bent head and thought silently:

'I'm going to make use of him. I'm going to take him as

the symbol of male nobility and compare his every word against my inner chaos. Why, just the other night I said God and no one answered me, not the way I like to be answered, with an assurance of compassion and tenderness. Spitting and hissing I get, but nothing else.'

The laughing village women had said to him: 'Tom! Tom! Come here and help us.'

'Why not I too?' she thought. She turned to him and said:

'Tom, you like to take care of people. Will you take care of me the way you care for others?'

Always wildly impulsive, he turned towards her so sharply, almost flinging his whole life into hers. Then he said with a still, cold intensity: '*Willingly*.'

Under other circumstances Dan would have been the perfectionist, the great teacher. He raked the personality over with the eyes of a hawk and grasped hold of all the weak spots. The great teachers had done the same. They had sent their mousy little disciples into corners shuddering with horror over character defects. But they had said, tenderly: 'Overcome the weakness, brother. Rise up from mouse to God.' The accent was on repairs, on gentle remodelling of personality.

Dan went as far as the hawk's eye. He saw in her a violent pride that could not endure humiliation of any kind. He saw the year behind of continuous unprovoked assault by Medusa and Sello of the brown suit. He saw the hidden molten lava within, the victim who is unreasonably tortured.

'Now I know what to do with that,' he said, triumphantly.

In a grand, superficial sort of way she could love an enemy, especially if he were big-hearted. It helped of course if the distances between them were immense, and knowing this she often turned to flight before her own hatred. It was often violent and final. In brooding solitude, she'd sort out the pros and cons. They were not often big-hearted. They were small, mean, petty, stifling souls.

'I'll never see so-and-so again. That solves it.'

It seemed to be a makeshift replacement for love, absenting oneself from stifling atmospheres, because love basically was a torrential storm of feeling; it thrived only in partnership with laughing generosity and truthfulness.

She could not sort out Sello, the shuttling movements he made between good and evil, the way he had introduced absolute perfection and flung muck in her face. Everything she knew of the living man was by hearsay. His other voice, so quietly, insistently truthful, barely rose above the high storm of obscenity. The two voices often seemed to merge, and a hawk's eye could easily sort out her own state of mind for her; it was both a sort of affection and a hatred for the man. The affection could be easily discounted, cast aside.

Dan wasn't only doing that with Elizabeth. He was applying the hawk's eye to Africa. The social defects he heightened in himself, then set himself up before Elizabeth as the epitome of the African male. She was later to cry out in agony:

'Oh, this filthy environment, where men sleep with the little girls they fathered, and other horrific evils.'

It was the power of his projection of his own personality as African. It began to make all things African vile and obscene. The social defects of Africa are, first, the African man's loose, carefree sexuality; it hasn't the stopgaps of love and tenderness and personal romantic treasuring of women. It is just sex, but it is not obscene because the women have a corresponding mental and physical approach.

The second social defect is a form of cruelty, really spite, that seems to have its origins in witchcraft practices. It is a sustained pressure of mental torture that reduces its victim to a state of permanent terror, and once they start on you they don't know where to stop, until you become stark, raving mad. Then they just grin.

He was a super-combination of both these defects, casting aside as useless the broad hazy body of social goodness and strength. To sex he added homosexuality and perversions of all kinds. To witchcraft terror he added the super-staying-power of his elemental soul; he could outlast anyone in a battle. All this he presented to Elizabeth.

Some years ago, Elizabeth had read through the two volumes of the Oscar Wilde trial, then after it picked up a biography on the man. The writer, a woman, sickened at the yapping of English society at his heels for his homosexual practices, said quietly: 'It doesn't matter where a man evacuates . . .' Elizabeth had accepted this as the final statement one could make on any deviate. It doesn't matter. It was one thing to adopt generous attitudes, at a distance. It was another to have a supreme pervert thrust his soul into your living body. It was like taking a walk on slime; slithering, skidding and cringing with a deep shame. It was like no longer having a digestive system, a marvellous body, filled with a network of blood-vessels – it was simply having a mouth and an alimentary tract; food was shit and piss; the sky, the stars, the earth, people, animals were also shit and piss. It was like living in the hot, feverish world of the pissing pervert of the public toilet – the sort of man who, in buses and cinema queues, pressed himself against a woman. And when a woman turned around and said: 'You shouldn't do that,' she looked right into a face with an uncomprehending smirk that said: 'But don't you like it? That's all I do. That's all I know. My whole life is my pissing vehicle. You're like that too. You're just pretending.'

It was as if people, ordinary normal people, lost their privacies to her. Two men gave her a lift that day into town when Dan turned on his homosexual record. He was anxious to impress upon Elizabeth that it was a universal phenomenon. The record said:

'They've tried it too. We all do. We try anything.'

The two men were friends. They cooked food together. They liked exotic recipes, and often tried to outdo each other in inventing new ones. One of the men had a giggle. The record said:

'You see, that's why he laughs like that.'

She sat in appalled, frozen silence between the two men. The record churned on and on. By night she was ill with the strain of it. It was as if Dan was setting the stage for his magnificent confession. That night in an awed voice and subdued whisper he introduced Mr Ghanzi and the great crisis in his life. He'd taken Mr Ghanzi to bed somewhere in the bush. He said to Elizabeth:

'I felt so ashamed, I nearly committed suicide. It doesn't happen between real men.'

Poor Mr Ghanzi had no pants on; his shirt-tails covered his thing. But he was standing in a field of flowers.

Then Dan said to Elizabeth: 'You are not supposed to think about it. It hurts me. I have to live inside you.'

That broke her. He had introduced his confession in such a pathetic voice her mind automatically jumped to defensive arguments: 'It's surely quite all right. I haven't any fixed opinions on this subject.' But the more she said it, the more a revulsion, an overpowering horror of men, arose in her. He was there all the time, watching her with still, steady eyes like a snake, ready to pounce at the right moment. He slipped in a second record:

'I only tried it once, but Sello keeps a full-time one. They do it all the time.'

With shaking hands she swallowed two sleeping-tablets and a glass of water. She thought she'd get some sleep. Instead, her mind swirled out into a vast horizon. Sello rose on it, very much as he had done in her first perception of him, but this time as a huge satanic personality. His face had greenish blotches on it, his mouth was a swollen mass of sensual depravity, his ears rose to sharp, pointed peaks. He was face to face with her. Like Thoko, who had suddenly been presented at her lands with the Mamba snake, she rolled out of the bed, flat on to the floor mat, dead with shock. A short while later her sanity returned. She thought about the monk sitting silently on the chair. She said loudly:

'Sello, are you really Satan?'

A deathly silence met her words.

She started muttering feverishly to herself. Something was giving way. She was really saying the opposite of what she was feeling. She was saying: 'God, Sello isn't Satan. He liked me, God. I don't mind bowing my head to the floor in memory of all the beautiful things he said. It was the woman who was so evil. Do you think I care about all the horrors that have been impressed upon me? I'm only sorry for all the suffering. I really like him too.'

To which God was she praying? She imagined she had control over her nervous system, she induced a false peace, she turned and crept back into bed. The huge satanic image seemed to be waiting for her full attention. He too turned. He had a rendezvous in mind. He was approaching his small girl, the one who had been holding on to his coffin. She raised one hand. She cried:

'Don't! Don't!'

At the same instant, Elizabeth shot wide awake. She looked in the dark at her clock. It was 3 a.m. She thought:

'If I don't close my eyes, I'll see no more of this.'

She sat up till dawn. The whole day her head pounded with pain. She reeled in a shut-in world of agony.

She sat up the whole of that night, not thinking, just staring at the dark with wide-open eyes. By midday the following day she started falling asleep on her feet. It was a Saturday afternoon. She managed to give the small boy some lunch. He ran up the road to the home of his playtime friends. He would not be back till sunset. She swallowed some more tablets and crept into bed. She blacked out. The nightmare crashed through her mental exhaustion. Dan, the master of this ceremony, stood over her in towering command.

'Come on,' he said wildly. 'Let go of him. You're holding on to his self-control. Let go. Let go.'

A filament-like umbilical cord suddenly appeared. Attached to its other end was Sello. The filament glowed with an incandescent light. As she looked at it, it parted in the middle, shrivelled and died. The huge satanic image of Sello opened its swollen, depraved mouth in one long scream. He staggered around like a drunk, then, like the demented Mr Hyde, jumped into his green truck and sped out of Motabeng village. Somewhere along the road he stopped his truck and made off, into the bush. A small boy was herding goats. He moved to attack him.

The Monday evening she turned on the radio, as she always did, for general news. A small boy had been found dead in the bush. He had been alone, herding goats. People always died in the bush, at the rate of two or three a month. It was full of wild animals and dangerous snakes. But this? But this? She began to believe her own nightmare. It was a combination of Dan and the hidden, molten lava. That was all he had waited for, the rise of the molten lava, a blind hatred of Sello. She thought a man like that ought really to die. She did not know Dan. He turned and pressed the intercom button to the boys downstairs and said:

'*Prepare da cement.*'

A belief in Sello's evil was to amount to a belief in the evil of a thousand people. He turned on the Sello drama thick, heavy and blow by blow.

Sello's small girl was in hospital with a nervous breakdown. The child was turning her head from side to side in agony. The word had got around the village, but he was a rich man; he could bribe anyone into silence. And what about his reputation as a prophet? The people were shaking their heads. There was a vivid picture of this. Then Dan burst out:

'He's shaken up! The prophecies aren't coming true! He's shaken up!'

He walked slowly towards Elizabeth. He had a concealed object in his hand. His whole face seemed to have turned into a seething, broiling, black storm. He said in a voice of deep menace: 'You see what you've collaborated with all this time?'

He raised his hand and struck her a blinding blow on the head. Her head exploded into a thousand fragments of fiery darkness. For two days she lay, barely conscious, in bed.

Kenosi came around. She sat down on a chair beside the bed. She was silent, self-contained, alertly practical. The drought-weather had broken in a terrible downpour. She said to Elizabeth: 'The water came into the garden. It has washed away one bed of tomatoes. I can see the place where the water came in through the fence. What must I do?'

Elizabeth could not raise her head.

'Where's Tom?' she whispered.

'He has gone away,' Kenosi said, impersonally.

'Can you dig a drain outside the fence?' Elizabeth said. 'The water will run down the drain instead of through the garden.'

'I can do it,' she said.

She sat looking at Elizabeth with her inscrutable expression.

'What's wrong with you?' she asked at last.

'I have 'flu,' Elizabeth said.

'You look very sick,' Kenosi commented.

She remained seated, her hands loosely folded in her lap. She did not seem to be feeling or thinking anything in particular. She just stared ahead of her solemnly. Suddenly she turned her head towards Elizabeth with a pretty appeal.

'You must never leave the garden,' she said. 'I cannot work without you. People are teasing me these days. They say: "Kenosi, where's your teacher? You are not in school." People have never seen a garden like our garden. It came there in one day.'

Elizabeth struggled to an upright posture. The way this woman brought her back to life and reality! Her head did not seem to be so full of splintered bone. She pushed back the bed-covers and stood up.

'I'll make tea,' she said smiling. 'Tomorrow I'll be back in the garden.'

Kenosi stirred a little, the gloom lifted from her face. The garden had become her whole life. She walked into it each day with softly swaying skirt and the movement and gestures of a woman taking care of all the detail of her household. She took on all the major tasks of bed preparation and worked with a deep concentrated intensity. Village women crowded around her, eager, curious. They knew cabbages and tomatoes. They were about the only vegetables that survived transport from Johannesburg. But what were green peas and the Lazy Housewife runner beans? How were they cooked? She turned to Elizabeth.

'People don't know all the new things we have here,' she liked to say, plaintively. 'The women say they can never buy the green peas.'

But in her eyes was the fierce glow of pride; the pride of the pioneer moving into the wonderful unknown.

It was like a scene from Macbeth or Hamlet in its weird morbidness. Sello sat on a chair in his house. A bell rang. He turned his head towards a door. His wife walked in.

'Is that the hospital?' he asked.

'No,' his wife said. 'It's the children.'

'Send them in,' he said.

Elizabeth looked at the wife. She was not smiling, but she walked with a careless swagger as though events of depravity were quite a common thing in her life. Elizabeth looked at Sello. His face was a frozen white mask, shrivelled and wizened like an old man's. A long line of village children filed in through the door. They were all chattering eagerly. Next to him Sello had a basin full of bread and jam. He handed each child a slice. They stood around eating with loud smacking noises. After all the bread had been handed out, he shooed them out of the room, then he turned to Elizabeth with a ghastly smile and said:

'You see, I am feeding all the children to make up for what happened last week.'

He stood up and with a slight limp walked slowly to a bed to lie down. As he lay down, Dan, who had been seated in a corner of the room, stood up and covered his whole form with a white sheet.

'Don't cover my poor small nose,' Sello giggled.

It was the first time they had appeared together in her nightmare. The funny reference to his nose was supposed to show jealousy of Dan's handsome big nose. It came over like that. Dan looked very aloof and coldly angry. Suddenly he turned to Elizabeth and in a voice of sharp command said:

'Lie down there!'

At first she moved towards the bed as an automatic response to a command, but as she sat on it it partly collapsed. She jumped to her feet and burst into tears. There was something horribly pathetic in the face of Sello. He also sprang off the bed. He looked from Dan to Elizabeth pleadingly and whimpered:

'They are going to kill me.'

Elizabeth increased her tears to a loud wail. She was deeply frightened. She saw out of the corner of one eye that Dan had moved and sat down on a chair. He leaned forward, his hands on his knees, his head bent in deep thought. Then he said, aloud to himself:

'How can I draw her?'

He stood up and looked quietly at Elizabeth. Sello was

trembling from head to foot and whimpering. She continued looking at Dan. He had won a total control of the situation. Every inch of him spelled outrage at Sello's evil. He was staring at Elizabeth in a strange way. It was not menacing and yet it was menace. It was too soft to be hatred and yet it was. It was the still, alert poise of a scorpion ready to strike. It was a silent assessment of Elizabeth. Did she really believe that Sello had molested his own child? Everything depended and hung on nightmare impressions. There wasn't any filth he couldn't cook up as long as he was sure of dominating the nightmare. He had begun to switch the emphasis. Sello had admitted to a thousand evils, but in a dim past, in civilizations of which there were no records left, because the order of that day had been a state where the power of the spirit had been openly used and misused and everything had ended in explosions. Sello had travelled back to that dim past, made the major admissions to himself and dragged Elizabeth along as an observer and revealed what he chose to reveal. There had been a little girl along that road who had rolled her eyes with a mock innocence, but children weren't made like that these days. They generally lived apart, in a world all their own, outside adult passions which were really incomprehensible to them. It was as though once the light had come it had closed the door on the darkness, and the courts of law took care of what remained in mankind's subconscious of all that horror. It wasn't for an individual to think out solutions to those problems, because it was so foreign to brood over her mind remained a total blank.

Ah, did she think she'd get off the hook so easily? Dan turned on a few records: The child is going to die. The child is going to commit suicide. What are you going to do about that?

To add to his drama, he had a slender, narrow, white coffin brought in and placed beside her. Still her mind refused to function. She could think of nothing as a comment on such a situation. But there were thousands of comments of children she knew; the way they talked all the time about their daily affairs:

'How old is Julius Caesar now?'

'If I go to Israel will I meet Moses?'

'Can I measure the moon?'

'You say there are fairies, well . . . I saw one.'

'You must build a chimney so that Father Christmas can come.'

'I deaded one of Mma-Taliman's chickens. Will she beat me?'

'Can I have five cents for sweets?'

'Can I go to the football match?'

'I don't want to go to bed. I'm still busy.'

'Tell me a story.'

. . . And so it went, on and on and on.

By Sunday of that week, Elizabeth had collapsed again. It really meant that she had come to accept the impossible, that Sello had molested his own child. Sello had said:

'You don't realize the point at which you become evil.'

For her, it was that point. Later she tried to make a thousand excuses for herself, through an inability to accept the doom of her inner nobility. But who had ever been faced with her circumstances? Who would ever agree that evil could be a powerful invasion force from outside? Who had ever had to live, over a period, with awful secrets and a nightmare like that, at once real and unreal?

'It wasn't my fault,' she said, over and over. 'I am not a tribal African. If I had been, I would have known the exact truth about Sello, whether he was good or bad. There aren't any secrets among tribal Africans. I was shut out from the everyday affairs of this world. Dan knew and traded on my ignorance. He did more. He struck me such terrible blows, the pain made me lose my mind.'

The only coherent thing about that Sunday was the small bird who lived in the tree outside her window. Somewhere near midday he began to sing to himself, a wobbly song of joy to the late rain of summer. It was always misty when he awoke in the morning these days, he said, and his tree-house dripped with moisture. As soon as the worms and beetles and ants crept out of the ground, he devoured them ravenously. A gorged gullet gave a fellow like him time now to reflect on the beauty of his surroundings. Then he suddenly shot up into a high note about the sparkling, rain-filled air. He held the high note beautifully for a full second.

She remembered thinking that some people die under beautiful circumstances, because the feverish pain in her head and limbs felt like a delirious, slowly-approaching death. She closed her eyes.

There was Dan. He was laughing, not a nice carefree laugh, but like the spider who has caught the fly. He showed her a rain of small rockets he'd apparently been pelting her with and implied that that was why she was feverish and ill. Then he said:

'I have a nice dinner for you.'

In walked Miss Body Beautiful. He had had to hold on to his thing all the time he was sitting on the judgement seat. It was time to relax. Body Beautiful had a grand introduction. She had long, straight, golden-brown legs. She raised her skirt a little and turned smiling black eyes on Elizabeth. Then there was a picture of her specialities. She had a brown chocolate cake, with creamy chocolate butter icing. Then he retreated in the dimness with his date. Suddenly he emerged again, panic-stricken. There was something fearfully wrong with Body Beautiful. He had in his hands a holy-water sprinkler such as the Roman Catholic priests use during high mass, and he solemnly raised the sprinkler and waved it around, God knows, perhaps blessing the environment. Some of the cool drops fell on Elizabeth. She could feel them like icy drops on her feverish body and soul. That was supposed to heal her. A part of her mind which was still a free observer of all this laughed with silent contempt. God, and any gesture towards the idea of God, stood clearly apart in her mind from all the gimmicks and foolery of the priests.

In any case, Dan was quite satisfied with his sprinkler. Now she could rise a bit and prepare lunch for the child. She was to find that Dan revelled in the vice-grip he had on her. The feeling was like that of Gulliver, pinned down to the ground with a thousand stakes. She was obviously nothing if his power could knock her over like that.

After lunch Elizabeth crawled back to bed.

There was Dan. His soul needed something ethereal. In sailed The Womb. She walked with her pelvis thrust forward and her feet shuffled in a jazzy rhythm along the floor. The ethereal part of it was that he was standing this time behind a curtain of light, to welcome her. She was the woman in the black silk dress who was to serve as the balance between Dan and Elizabeth because his soul was too powerful for direct contact with Elizabeth. She swished aside the curtain of light and entered full of confidence. Apparently there was a network of light joining them all together, and because of this events behind the curtain were gorgeous. At the end of it, he charmingly confided in Elizabeth: The Womb made this thing jump up and down. She had a womb he could not forget. Then he turned on his records:

You are supposed to feel jealous.

I go with all these women because you are inferior. You cannot make it up to my level because we are not made the same way.

At the same time he kept, switched on, the almost still-life picture of Sello's small girl with her angelic face turned up in a posture of death. It hung over Elizabeth like the sword of Damocles.

By Monday morning, Elizabeth was very alert mentally. This was hell proper. The depths of the man were so awful that she simply disliked him and wanted to pull her mind out of the chaos. So closely did he keep up a running commentary on all her feelings that he was prepared for this. He came rushing towards her like a violent windstorm, full of sand and swirling dust. Everything seemed about to disappear under the impact of the storm.

'It's over,' he said. 'It's over. If you leave me I'll die, because I have nothing else.'

How many records he had ready to turn on like that, with the creepy pathetic undertone of, supposedly, a great love they had hidden away together in some dim past. She ought to be loyal to it, never betray it. He jumped like that to the universal all-embracing past of love where, apparently, it had not mattered if they were separate races or not, as they were now – he was African, she was mixed breed. What a plague that was! Perhaps in their past incarnations as lovers they had mercifully been of the same race and could peacefully join their souls together 'at the roots'?

Something clearly emerged as she reflected back. The man

took her for a damn fool. He staged any kind of show, down to the level of her reasoning. Sello, who had put up a terrific performance as a pervert, quietly exited. He was to reappear with his boy-friend. Dan had an interval show to put up with the girls. Who were they? Miss Pelican-Beak, Miss Chopper, Miss Pink Sugar-Icing, whom he was on the point of marrying, Madame Make-Love-On-The-Floor where anything goes, The Sugar-Plum Fairy, more of Body Beautiful, more of The Womb, a demonstration of sexual stamina with five local women, this time with the lights on, Madame Squelch Squelch, Madame Loose-Bottom – the list of them was endless. But there was a short lull before all this. He caught hold of Elizabeth's hand to show her what linked them together, eternally – that exquisite sensation no other man gave her. It came like a steady vibration from his hand to her hand. Was she satisfied? He was giving her so much! Few women were in the position of getting a vibration like that. Oh no, Elizabeth was ungrateful. She had lived a life other than this, where her soul was her own, and the peace within had let her mind meander on all sorts of dreamy pathways. She had writers she loved, and had kept their books beside her bed and each night read and re-read their most glorious soaring passages. They seemed to grow old with her, and only as her mind matured did a comprehension of their struggles and efforts grow as a living reality in her own mind. She had tried to pick up those books, but between her and the written words reeled Dan's terrible records:

He's a homosexual, he also sleeps with cows and anything on earth.

Who was saying this to whom? Both he and Sello seemed to be saying this to each other; they had become merged as horrors in her mind.

The elegant pathway of private thought, like the wind sweeping around a bend in the unknown road of the future, had been entirely disrupted. The steady peace and stability of soul had been blasted away and replaced by a torrent of filth. She was not supposed to sort out one thing from another. Dan had set her up as the queen of passive observation of hell. Who else received such an honour? It was so stunning that in the dark of the night she turned her face to the wall and cried, a long impromptu wail of agony:

'God, what is happening to me? What have I done in the past to suffer so much? I haven't had time in the present to commit great evils. People born with no parents to care for them are extra alert about the dangers of life. You know that man, Woody? I'm sorry I kissed Woody, who was married. That's the only really bad thing I did, but I kissed him because we had been friends for a long time. And even then he could not kiss nicely at all. It was soggy and wet and I never bothered to kiss him again. I can't think of any other bad things except pinching some underarm perfume from a shop once, for which I'm also sorry....'

And so on and so on. Only the insects in the dark night talked also to themselves in long, brooding, plaintive soliloquies. Dan listened for a time to these soliloquies to God, the wall. So, she didn't care a hell about that vibration he'd pumped into her hand? It was extra special stuff. He parted with it sparingly. He began banging things around, violently.

'I can't stand it!' he shouted. 'I can't stand this moaning!'

He was stampeding off somewhere. He looked like he really was, the super-slick Casanova who knew all about the girls. Couldn't she see the angry handsome profile, the expensive suit? He, the king of women, had condescended to associate with low trash – and how subtly he always conveyed her inferiority to her in ways like this. His conscience must have been troubling him too; any fool could have seen through his cooked-up plot against Sello, so he switched the emphasis – it all lay on her rejection of his vibration. She had to pay for it, and pay for it through feverish nights of insomnia, when his activities with the girls crashed through heavy doses of sleeping-tablets. Do they ever go away when they are explicitly there to exploit and use their victims? They spit so hard at what they despise, but they stay until they have sucked all life dry, until all is desolation.

It wasn't any kind of physical stamina that kept her going, but a vague, instinctive pattern of normal human decencies combined with the work she did, the people she met each day and the unfolding of a project with exciting inventive possibilities. But a person eventually becomes a replica of the inner demons he battles with. Any kind of demon is more powerful than normal human decencies, because such things do not exist for him.

When a man is born to create beautiful dreams he seems in every way mentally prepared for the event. The Eugene man stood before a crowd of people, a mingling of the teachers from the Motabeng Secondary School and villagers who had come to the opening day of the local-industries project shop. He waved his hands diffidently, blinked his eyes and spoke in a soft, offhand voice:

'Everybody knows that the things we have in our store we have made with our own hands. A small handful of members have shown considerable faith in the concept of establishing local industries. They have worked patiently without reward to produce these goods. Our shop is owned by its members. We pool and share all our resources; we mutually depend on each other for employment and through such co-operation we learn new skills. One member of each group will give a brief explanation or demonstration of the work they have done to produce the goods for our store.'

He stepped aside. The producers of the rough home-made articles sat to one side, apart from the visitors. From among them a young girl stood up and stepped into a cleared, central area. She was very pretty and full of self-confidence. She wore on her person all the articles the sewing-group had produced up to date. With delightful gestures, she modelled a blue and white polka-dot loose shift dress, then from her arm she held up a shopping bag woven together in a fancy design from rough, coarse string; and around her neck was a necklace she had made from the seeds of the Morake tree.

'We make dresses, shopping bags and necklaces,' she said, smiling prettily. Then sat down. There was a murmur of approval, no doubt in favour of the extreme prettiness of the girl.

A potter's wheel was pulled to the centre of the clearing, and again a young girl stepped forward and sat on the projecting seat attached to the wheel. She placed beside her a small bucket of water and from her left hand threw a lump of wet clay on to the wheel. Then she lightly sprinkled the clay with water and pressed her fóot on a pedal beneath the wheel. With a shy concentration, she quickly moulded the clay into a vase, then stood up and pointed to a shelf on which were arranged the goods of the pottery work-group. They were thick, chunky, heavy household crockery, finished off with brilliant glazes and local designs of wild flowers and wild animals.

'We make teasets, plates, mugs, jugs, ashtrays, bowls and flower vases,' she said.

An old man shuffled forward. He blinked his eyes mistily and said, haltingly: 'I make bricks from earth and sand. I burn the bricks in a kiln.'

He held up a burnt, reddish-brown brick. His kiln was just outside the garden fence. All day long he shuffled around his kiln, unheedful of the other activities around him. Elizabeth adored simply standing still a few moments and watching him shuffle to and fro with his bricks, as though bricks had been all his life was composed of. Kenosi had told her that the old man had really been the fence-maker of the village – when people set up their houses he had built their fences – and then late in life he had changed to brick-making, maybe out of an eagerness to do something new.

Kenosi stepped forward next with an explanation of the garden work. She slightly averted her head from the audience and said, softly: 'I work in the garden with Elizabeth. We grow all kinds of vegetables.'

She paused and pointed to a shelf on which was a heaped-up pile of brilliantly green cabbage-heads, tomatoes, green beans and carrots – their first harvest. How people liked vegetables! A murmur of approval went up. She next brought a box filled with earth to the centre and, like a magician, picked up a huge cabbage seedling growing in a plastic bag filled with soil. She said:

'We grow all our tomato and cabbage seedlings in plastic bags. It is the easiest method of transplanting. Our seedlings do not wilt or die because they are so strong.'

She raised the seedling in its soil bag in her hand. Next, she scooped out a hole in the soil with a hand shovel; then with a razor slit the sides of the plastic, and in her hands was a solid mould of earth. She placed the soil mould with its quivering head of bright green leaves into the hole and pressed and smoothed over the soil in the box around it. Well ... then how often could Elizabeth advertise her instant garden of gigantic cabbage seedlings? As if this were not enough, they had the Cape Gooseberry too, another miracle-performer. Kenosi said:

'In our garden we also grow the Cape Gooseberry and use the fruit to make jam.'

She walked to a shelf and picked up a bottle filled with golden, whole-fruit gooseberry jam. Again a murmur of approval swept the crowd. Some of the village women laughed. The whole village had been subjected to a battery of propaganda leaflets distributed by Kenosi and Elizabeth about the usefulness and prolific fruit-bearing properties of the Cape Gooseberry. At first, the miracle had occurred in Elizabeth's yard. She had planted out fifty seedlings. Over a period of three months they had slowly developed into shrubs, two feet high. One day, as she walked through her garden she noted thick mats of brown husks lying on the ground beneath the gooseberry bushes. With Kenosi, she harvested an enormous basket of berries, not only berries but a heavenly view of glistening autumn shades of brown, yellow-gold, green-tinted fruit. The fruit in the basket weighed ten pounds. It was the desert surroundings of Motabeng that made them stare so incredulously at the huge harvest. The following week they harvested another ten pounds. And it looked as if this harvest of ten pounds of fruit a week would continue for an indefinite period. At first Elizabeth sold all the fruit to the teachers' wives of Motabeng Secondary School in sheer panic at having so much fruit on her hands. By the fourth week, she had gathered her wits together and also gathered whatever information was available on the Cape Gooseberry – the jam Grahame had mentioned, here was the jam for the local-industries shop! The roneoed sheets of paper went speeding through the village. Everyone had to know. Elizabeth wrote:

'We have a large vegetable garden in the valley, a part of the local-industries project. In our garden we are going to plant a great number of Cape Gooseberry bushes. We would like to sell the fruit of the Cape Gooseberry to housewives as it makes a very tasty jam, which is simple and easy to prepare. The Cape Gooseberry is also a good health food for the family as it is rich in Vitamin C, which helps prevent skin ailments like scurvy. We therefore hope the little children will patronize us and come to favour the Cape Gooseberry above the varieties of wild bush berries which they now eat and which cannot be so nutritious . . .' The introduction was followed by a recipe for Cape Gooseberry Jam.

The village women always passed by Elizabeth's house to collect firewood in the bush. If they saw her in the yard, they stopped, laughed and said: 'Cape Gooseberry', to show how well they had picked up the propaganda. They did it so often that eventually Elizabeth became known as 'Cape Gooseberry'.

The work had a melody like that – a complete stranger like the Cape Gooseberry settled down and became a part of the village life of Motabeng. It loved the hot, dry Botswana summers as they were a replica of the Mediterranean summers of its home in the Cape.

An old lady who next stepped forward had a similar tale to tell about the wool she had used for the poncho or shawl she was modelling. The wool work-group had their own imported Merino sheep which were being reared on the school farm. They had sheared the sheep themselves and cleaned, spun and woven the wool, and after it had been dyed they had made shawls, floor-mats, blankets and jerseys on simple home-made looms.

The cynical-eyed villagers listened to all these explanations of productivity with reserve. They were the last people on earth to be told about how to work and produce things with their own hands; they did that all the time. They gathered the earth together and built it up into solid walls of mud for their homes; they felled trees in the bush for the supports and rafters of their roofs and cut the long, rough wild grass for their thatch. They knew about living on nothing. The local-industries people were doing an extension of their tough, severe subsistence living. Not one person had walked home with money after all this labour, and that was what they wanted to know about. They were just poor people like everyone else, and from the pathetic appearance of the crude goods in the shop it seemed unlikely they would ever become millionaires.

But, all the same, people who say they have something to peddle or sell always find people who'll buy. The villagers stood up eagerly once the shop had been declared open, searched around in their purses for meanly hoarded coins and in a twinkling bought up all the cabbages, green beans, carrots and gooseberry jam; the teachers of Motabeng school bought all the pottery, floor-mats and woollen blankets. Crude candles, washing soap and lanoline also disappeared, and since the shoppers were thirsty they stood around drinking bottles of weak, watery cold drink made from orange powder and called 'Fanta'. By the end of the day, the producers looked at a shop that had been stripped almost bare of goods. A Motabeng teacher quickly coined a joke for this situation.

'Here,' he said, 'we have too many people chasing too few goods.'

And so the local-industries project was born, and the valley area became a quiet hum of activity:

Tshipi Ya Dikgomo – We Brand Your Cattle, said a huge notice board in an open space.

We Buy Fowls

We Buy Goats

We Sell Bricks

Try Our Marang – The Dawn, Lager Beer Brewed in Botswana

We Deliver Water and Firewood, right to your homes

Bring All Your Laundry To Us

'Sister' sells Fat Cakes, Ginger Beer and 'Fanta' in the store

Visit Our Pottery House

Our Builders Can Build Your Homes

And so on. New activities and work-groups were being formed each day as the activities came to mind. For the members, it was a school where they learnt, in simple form, the basic workings of productivity. On the first Saturday morning after the store had opened, a shares and price meeting was held. The members all crowded into the store and sat down on the floor. They were handed roneoed sheets of paper on which was an analysis of the week's production and earnings:

NUMBER OF PEOPLE	WORK-GROUP	TOTAL EARNINGS
4	Garden	R10.00
3	Brick Making	R10.50
3	Water Delivery	R6.00
2	Firewood Delivery	R6.00
1	Laundry	R5.00
1	Soap Making	R2.00
5	Weaving & Spinning	R15.50
5	Sewing	R3.50
3	Cooking	R4.00
3	Lager Beer	R4.00
4	Pottery	R12.00
2	Cold Drinks	R1.50
40		R80.00

The Eugene man stood before a blackboard.

'We have R80.00 to share among forty people,' he said. 'That means each member may take home R2.00 each. Is this what we do?'

An old woman spoke up quickly and scornfully:

'That's what we call working for death. When money comes into our house, we use half and save half. If we eat all that money, then local-industries people are just working for death.'

There was an instantaneous agreement about this, yet it provoked a general philosophical discussion among the members. A little money saved was the central part of village life. The sale of three goats and a cow brought in the major income for the year, and out of this a little was set aside for household needs and a little saved, because a thousand disasters and debts of an unexpected nature arose before the time came when a man was prepared or able to sell another beast. The local-industries people were on the whole so poor that they did not even have a goat to sell – drought and loss through drought had taken care of that – but they still applied the finances of village life to their project. To sum up the discussion, a middle-aged woman said, with a profound air of wisdom:

'We would like to take home more money, but as people have said, sewing-group will need material, garden-group will soon need more seed and for the kitchen and restaurant we have to purchase a stove and chairs and tables. All this we have to purchase from our savings, so we are all agreed to take home R1.00 and save R1.00 for our needs.'

Once the agreed sum of R1.00 each had been distributed among all the members, the price meeting began.

'We have noticed that people take a long time to make things,' Eugene said, 'and this makes the cost of the goods higher.'

He paused and held up a bright floral pillow:

'Let us make a breakdown of the selling price of this pillow, showing how much it cost us to make.' He turned to the board and wrote:

Cost of raw cotton, with seed (1lb)		.05c
Cost of labour to clean cotton		R1.50
Cost of covering material		.67
	Total cost	R2.22
Plus 25% mark up to cover expenses & profit		.55c
	Selling price	R2.77

There was a moment's silence. The villagers concentrated intently on the figures on the blackboard, then an old man said: 'Yes, people have observed that our prices are far too high. Why is the price so high?'

'Because it took five girls six days to clean the cotton wool,' Eugene replied. 'If it takes so long to clean one pound of cotton wool, then someone has to suffer, as we are producers who want a market for our goods.'

'Who takes so long to clean cotton wool?' the old man asked, indignantly. 'Name these people.'

'They are the sewing-group,' a woman piped up.

The poor victims did not know where to hide their faces. It caused such a commotion that everyone started talking at once, and an old woman's voice rose high and shrill over the rest:

'There are too many people loafing around here,' she said. 'We tell them to work and they say they are just resting a little because they cannot work so hard.'

A woman sitting next to Elizabeth countered with:

'That's not the real truth. People here are stubborn and proud because of their 25c shares. They paid 25c and were told they were the owners of the work. When they are told to work they say: "What? If there's any nonsense around here we will just take our 25c shares and go home." There is no one who can control them because they have been told that they are owners of everything around here.'

They were still muttering like that when an old man stood up slowly and importantly. People thought he had a momentous speech to make on production and turned to him, expectantly. He said: 'Last week I fell off a lorry. . . .'

He got no further than that. A loud roar of laughter from the audience drowned the remainder of his words. He stood there smiling good-humouredly. He had broken the serious, tense atmosphere of the schoolroom. As people walked out, they looked at the blackboard and shook their heads. An old woman remarked:

'At my age, I am far too old to return to school again. Yo!'

If such a beauty and harmony built up in her outward circumstances it was at total odds with the tormented hell of her inner world. That was supposed to be momentous too. She was supposed to be observing the immense stature and power of a soul who was really God but who had failed to get the prophecies. Half her attention was turned towards the daily round of a vegetable gardener's life, which is full of people. The ladies of the village came down to the garden with baskets on their arms. They always wanted spinach and cabbage. Each year during the rainy season they collected a wild variety in the bush, dried it and carefully preserved it for use over the long dry season when not a green thing was in sight. Here in the garden were crisp, juicy leaves of Swiss Chard, Collards from America and perpetual spinach beet. To Elizabeth's surprise, the English volunteers were just as mad about vegetables as were the village ladies. They liked to walk up and down the garden, their hands behind their backs with amazed expressions on their faces.

'Elizabeth,' they said, 'you can't grow green peas like that in England. You can't ever find the green peas among all the weeds that come up.' And, 'Your Cape Gooseberry isn't at all like the English gooseberry. The taste is different, and ours are hairy.' And, 'You know, Elizabeth, this is one story I have to take back to England – Sweet Peppers for 5c a pound! They're so rare in England they cost as much as steak!'

There were a thousand such stories to tell of life in Motabeng, of tentative efforts people of totally foreign backgrounds made to work together and understand each other's humanity; that needed analysing – intangible, unpraised efforts to establish the brotherhood of man. A young man had recently come over from London to start work in the brewery house of the local-industries project. Since he also liked to walk up and down the garden and stare at everything, Elizabeth soon became friendly with him. He had taken up lodgings in a mud hut with a local family, just over the road from Elizabeth's house, and one evening he invited her to have supper with him. He sat in his small mud hut, on a low, hand-carved stool, neatly pressed his long legs together and looked around his home with immense pleasure, and remarked:

'This is the first home I've had to myself in all my life.'

He had a small pot of rice cooking by an outdoor fireplace, and every now and then Elizabeth ran out into the dark to observe how the rice was getting along. The fireplace belonged to his landlady, and she sat unconcernedly with her family on a mat outside her hut drinking tea, as though foreigners and local people had always shared outdoor fires. When Elizabeth re-entered the hut, the young man said:

'I'm not too happy about the arrangement here. I offered to pay R2 a month for my hut but the family refused to accept it. They said I should help them and they would help me. I share some of my food with them, but it doesn't quite work out the right way, and I'd be happy to pay the money. Could you sort it out for me?'

'I'll find out,' Elizabeth promised. 'I know the woman. We used to make seedlings together.'

When the woman was questioned she replied that it was a kindness to a person who was a foreigner; but the story went a little deeper than that. People believe in tenderness, especially in tender heavens of compassion. These belonged to a God in the sky who would do everything for the poor in some magical way. It was quite another thing to be loved and cared for in a realistic way by other living people who came from London. These things had to be enquired into by the poor; so they opened their doors to the volunteers who wanted to live among them, so that they could comprehend a new world that had suddenly made them precious, valued.

Elizabeth was never to regain a sense of security or stability on the question of how patterns of goodness were too soft, too indefinable to counter the tumultous roar of evil. Why else was that whole year lost to her, when so much of life around her unfolded with beautiful harmony? Why did she keep on stumbling down to the garden with the roar of hell in her ears:

'When I go I go on for one hour. . . .'

Before her gaze, Dan's head exploded into a ball of that red fire. The loud, pounding rhythm of his drama drummed in her ears day and night. It was like large, grasping hands gathering every thread of her life to themselves for a total command; a total encroachment on her mind and soul. He behaved as though he were giving her a supreme education into facts of life that had totally escaped her notice. A persistent theme was that she was not genuinely African; *he* had to give her the real African insight. People in her daily life were vividly reintroduced through imagery at night. In almost every way she had slighted somebody. In almost every way she had to be aware of Africans as a special holy entity and deep mystery he alone understood. He too was a deep mystery she would never fathom. He could so subtly play on the earlier themes Sello had introduced to her mind about the poor, their central importance, and yet he twisted and perverted these themes with a merciless cruelty. A poor woman would be introduced with her simplicity and abysmal poverty. Then he had a story about how she spent her nights; her children slept with her in the same hut where she made love with men.

'It hurts the children,' he moralized piously.

He'd pick on people she met in daily life, always introducing a vivid, indelible fact about their sex lives, so abruptly, so unexpectedly that her daily contacts were reduced to that one fact. The persistent picking on people she met in her daily life totally demoralized her, as though Dan were saying:

'You see, your eyes are my eyes, but I know and see more than you.' He was the great informant on hidden things. There wasn't any detail of her contacts with people left innocent and normal; everything was high, sexual hysteria. The hot, feverish soul of the man totally broke and bent her. When she did not take tablets to counter the high, screaming hysteria, she turned around and snapped at people, and often walked blindly past them without returning greetings. Only one relationship escaped a head-on verbal explosion. It was her relationship with Kenosi. He meddled there too. But the woman lived her own shut-in, elusive life, and the work-relationship had been established on the solid respect of one work partner for another. As the year once more came to an end, this time in a tumultuous roar of mental confusion, she made every effort to avoid turning around and snapping at Kenosi too, until she was forced into total silence. All Kenosi did was stare back at her with an inscrutable, severe expression.

Nothing stood between her and her observations of Dan. It was like the rabbit trapped in helpless fascination by the powerful downward swoop of the hawk. It knows its death is near and awaits it, helplessly.

He picked on Tom, too, but Dan didn't wish to overstrain Elizabeth's gullibility. Tom, he said carefully, had the potential to be a homosexual, but he wasn't yet; and obligingly, in her nightmare, there was Tom stuttering: 'The dormitories . . . The dormitories.' When Tom wasn't away in some other village investigating the possibilities of expanding the farmers' youth-development work-groups, he kept his lodgings with the farm students of the Motabeng project. He also kept up his friendship with Elizabeth. It was the sort of friendship where anything had been and could be discussed without creating embarrassment, and so demented was she by the torture of these obscene hisses that when Tom next called around she actually turned to him and asked:

'Tom, what's your attitude towards homosexuals?'

'Whatever makes you think of that, Elizabeth?' he asked, instantly surprised. 'There aren't any gays around here. The last time I saw a gay was in America. This is one of the most unobscene societies in the world. Men just sleep with women, and that's all there is to it.'

She laughed a bit. The world steadied itself.

'What did you say, Tom?' she said, distracted by the term 'gay'. It was suddenly so apt. The funny men fluttered their eyes in mock imitation of women's gestures. 'What was that about "gay"?'

'We call them gay guys,' he said, laughing. 'They're pretty. They're women.'

'What would you do if a gay approached you?'

He turned and looked at her seriously: 'I'd be offended,' he said.

'Tom,' she persisted. 'What would you do if you were both God and Satan at the same time?'

He took this question equally seriously, and bent his head for a moment in deep thought. Then he said:

'I hope I'd have the courage to admit it to myself.'

'You wouldn't want anyone else to know?' she asked anxiously. 'You'd want it to be a secret?'

'Yes,' he said. 'Because it's such a terrible idea.'

'But it's possible, isn't it?' she persisted. 'The dividing line between good and evil is very narrow.'

'Yes,' he said, quietly. Then he turned and looked at her with an expression of deep affection. He was a very outpouring sort of person. He sensed the inward, reeling confusion in her. He reached out with a thick, grubby hand and touched the back of her neck. She kept quiet, but her shattered mind was screaming aloud in agony: 'Sello is prancing around in my nightmare with his face full of swollen green blotches. There's a little girl with her face upturned in death. And last night Madame Make-Love-On-The-Floor just raised her legs high in the air. There's no escape for me. There's nothing I can do to stop it. I'm going insane.'

It was the last coherent conversation she had with him, because when he returned in November she was stark, raving mad. He was sitting at the table. He'd said something about his work and she turned on him and burst out into a tirade against the Ku Klux Klan. He sat quite still and listened to the tirade then stood up and said with a cold hostility:

'You don't have to tell me anything about America. I know all about it. I know about Americans who come over here and just remain big, stupid Americans. Nothing changes them. . . .' His voice broke a little as though he were about to cry. He stood up and walked out.

It was about September that she retained her last coherent memory of the activities in the garden. An art teacher from the Secondary School had for about three weeks been after an enormous cauliflower as a model for a still-life art lesson. There had been a battle to prevent its being sold to other customers who also watched it with voracious eyes; there'd been the fascination of watching it swell and swell to a huge white cloud of food. It was so big when finally picked that the art teacher had to hold it in both her arms. She had turned triumphant blue eyes on Elizabeth and laughed as though obtaining the cauliflower had been the greatest achievement of her life. It lived there in Elizabeth's memory, the young woman embracing a cauliflower as big as her chest.

When someone knows they are failing in every way, they still keep up the routine, filling in the gaps and blanks with frantic efforts to regain a health and control that aren't there. She only had to work with Kenosi in the garden till midday. The whole afternoon she worked in her own yard, which was the great experimental centre where everything new was tried out; and after the Cape Gooseberry they were always trying out something new, and someone was always turning up with the seed of a miracle food-producer. They'd say to Elizabeth: 'I wrote to a friend about your garden and she sent me this tomato seed. "Indian River" it's called. She said they had a drought and it spoilt their orange plantation. They wanted to make up with a quick cash crop and produced a bumper harvest with the "Indian River". She writes that it grows to a height of five feet with fruit all the way down the vine, and I thought that's just what Elizabeth would like. Try some of this seed.'

So tobacco, tomatoes, broccoli, peanuts all grew happily side by side in her garden. Tobacco was for snuff, peanuts for cooking oil and peanut butter, tomatoes were 'specialities' and broccoli might just like to grow in Motabeng. Records were kept of ailments, growth and food production, and after all was well the 'specialities' were transferred to the local-industries garden. Many people were involved in the inventive genius of that garden, many people turned up with seed, even at one time some Weevil-ridden barley they persuaded Kenosi to plant in Elizabeth's absence. She had listened to Kenosi's plaintive voice, and in a dim haze of pain examined the bag of what was left over of the barley.

'Look at what Rodney did to me,' Kenosi said. 'He made me plant this rotten barley. I was afraid to refuse because people like to help, and they complain about me to Eugene when I say they are messing up the work.'

'Never mind,' Elizabeth had replied. 'Let's dig up that bed and plant carrots. When Rodney comes again tell him the carrots are barley. He doesn't know anything about vegetables because he teaches history.'

She struggled to hold on to the morning's work, with all its humour and weird drama, but the afternoons, which were set aside for seedling work and 'specialities', she began to reserve for collapses.

'If I rest a little my legs won't feel so lame, the pain in my head will go away, then at five I'll plant out some new seed and water the garden,' she'd think.

Everything she thought out suited the plans of Dan. After all, he was only there to kill her. It was taking so long, the road was so devious, his activities so tremendous. The weaker she became, the more intensely excited did he become, something like the way animals scent blood or death in the air.

The seventy-one nice-time girls appeared at some stage or another to have fallen prostrate at Dan's feet, never to rise again. They mingled and moved together before Elizabeth's gaze, their one common bond being their blind adoration of Dan. They displayed no particular jealousy or hostility towards each other, but to Elizabeth they all invariably turned with that mocking smile she had first seen on the face of Medusa – they had what she had not got. It was only now and then that Dan appeared enslaved. Madame Loose-Bottom had a sexual potency on a scale ten times greater than Dan's. He would go into a bottomless pit of insatiability. Her symbol was a clump of wild grass, her sex was like a rough tumble in the wilderness. For a little, while she moved haughtily, arrogantly before Elizabeth, she was the nearest equal he had had to Sello's Medusa. Some of them made him panic a little. She did. And Body Beautiful did. Their sex must not be a little more than he could manage. Also women more sexually potent than he were incredibly 'dirty'. He unfolded a long story about Madame Loose-Bottom. She was a fallen goddess; her fall had been so bad that she was the sort of woman who had slept with her own sons. He said: 'Her past was so bad that even the police could not keep records of it.'

Well, he went with Madame Loose-Bottom for some nights, then decided that there must be an end to her. He suddenly grabbed hold of her and brought her face to face with Elizabeth. This was most probably meant to be a soul-confrontation of evil with good, because as Elizabeth looked at her she slowly dissolved into nothing.

The next thing he could not stand was the orgasm of Body Beautiful. It was feverish and hysterical and apparently affected him in a painful way. She was made to expose everything. The flesh of her private parts had a raw, red look as though the surface skin had been rubbed off by many hands. Like a small child wetting her pants, she had an orgasm right on top of Elizabeth. The following day Elizabeth tried to rise out of bed and collapsed again with a high, delirious fever.

'It's all right,' she heard Dan say. 'You've taken it away.'

If that were so, it explained his first panic at going with Body Beautiful. She had given him such a shock that he had sprinkled his surroundings with the holy-water sprinkler.

Another girl who was a bit too much for him was Madame Squelch Squelch. Her whole pelvis area was molten lava. Her symbol was darkness. He so despised her that he made short work of her. Of her he said: 'She's so uncontrolled that she just goes all the time.'

He did a few limbering up exercises, then went with Squelch Squelch. It was so awful for him – after all, he was God – that he threw up after the job. The main thing was that, in the process of going with her, he had cleaned her up, he had made her impotent. She kindly exposed a spotless vagina right in Elizabeth's face.

The Sugar-Plum Fairy was the great goddess. In all the hell of his harem she was the delicate, beautiful, ethereal soul. She had principles and nobility. She was so upper-class that really to go with Dan was, for her, coming down to slumming level. After all, hadn't Lady Chatterley done it? That seemed to be the summary of their relationship. Here he created a great crisis for himself. He had to give up this delicate goddess for the sake of Elizabeth. Would the Sugar-Plum Fairy agree? They were talking it over together, and Elizabeth was made to overhear. The Sugar-Plum said:

'If you ever want me, I'll come to you secretly.'

Sugar-Plum seemed to revel in tortured love affairs; this seemed to have been the pattern of their relationship in their past lives. Dan was always the hopeless outsider given crumbs by the lady, and it seemed a sweet anguish to the lady to tear herself between the grand Lord she usually married and Dan whom she loved, then didn't love, then loved. Presumably this kind of anguish had heightened their love, made it terribly sacred, holy and beautiful. She looked just like a true-romance story from a woman's magazine. In spite of the delicate construction of the lady's soul, Dan confided to Elizabeth an astounding detail. She was always ready to 'go'. She was very obliging about this in a quiet lady-like way.

The Womb, one of his favourites, had to be made a little classy. She'd achieve this classiness by taking some of Elizabeth's dresses for her own. The dresses had acquired a symbolic meaning. There was one with bright, multicoloured floral patterns. It was symbolic of appeal, creativity and vitality, he said. The dress had to be given to The Womb because she had acquired a greater status than Elizabeth. She had contractions in her womb that were so exciting, and ah, he was so charmed by them! For some reason, The Womb was terribly scared to just go and take the dress. She hesitated and looked at Elizabeth with a gleam of fear in her eyes, then crawled down on the floor and crept stealthily to the wardrobe. Dan dimmed the lights. In the early morning he was caressing the soft, drooping breast of The Womb. She wore Elizabeth's dress.

Then he had a dramatic announcement to make. For some time he had been engaged to marry Miss Pink Sugar-Icing. She was the daughter of one of his wealthy friends. All Motabeng village knew about the engagement, except Elizabeth. Apparently this was a marriage of convenience. He told Elizabeth he supported a lot of poor relatives, and the girl's income from her rich parents would ease his burden. Pink Sugar-Icing had no physical specialities, except that to go with her was like eating sponge cake with pink sugar-icing; that was her symbol. She had long, thin, delicate hands with pointed, manicured fingernails. She'd never done a bit of work in her life, and her hands were so soft they looked as though they had only picked flowers. She had a wifely interest in Dan, however. She approached Elizabeth and asked with a friendly smile: 'Do you know Dan?'

Not quite knowing how to reply to this, Elizabeth instead pointed to a record in Pink Sugar's hand.

'What do you have there?' she asked her.

'It's the record of Dan's life,' Pink Sugar said. 'He's had a lot of affairs.'

She handed the long-playing record to Elizabeth. It had some jazz numbers Elizabeth knew: April In Paris, Autumn in New York ...

'They can be very soft, beautiful pieces,' Elizabeth said, smiling.

'Oh, you just have to hear them,' Pink Sugar laughed. 'You won't like them at all.'

Elizabeth turned to a record-player at her side. The first number she played was: April In Paris. It was the favourite of thousands of jazz men, but instead of the familiar soft, low blend of the double bass, drums and piano, a chorus of women screeched: 'April in Paris, what have you done to my heart, giggle, giggle, giggle. ...'

She quickly took off the record.

'You see,' said Pink Sugar. 'That goes on all the time, and we're supposed to be getting married in December, you know.'

He went with Miss Pink Sugar-Icing for a few nights, but in spite of her wealth and promise of security for his poor relatives, she was very boring. He dropped her abruptly and introduced Miss Pelican-Beak. In every way Pelican-Beak was enchantment. She was gay and carefree, tough, energetic and so athletic she seemed to be a trapeze artist. Her symbol came along with her, the beak of the Pelican bird. It referred to her passageway, which was long and tough like the bird's beak. This special gift enabled her to make love in all sorts of postures without any danger of internal injury; that is, she could twist her legs above her head, she could twist this way and that, she could do all sorts of things, and, like Miss Sewing-Machine, go the whole night and wake up the next morning with no ill-effects. She had spindly bony knees and elbows, and thrust her elbows out to show that she usually pushed everyone else out of the way. Nothing stood between her and her desires.

With an enchanting smile, she displayed before Elizabeth a number of coloured panties, black, pink, blue, yellow. Briskly the black pantie went sailing away into the night. She did not need it. The gentleman dimmed the lights but, as at the times he went with Miss Sewing-Machine, they kept on bumping her awake with their activities. And Miss Pelican-Beak liked to make comments like 'Don't!', as though she were suddenly ashamed of something because it was love-making with all the stops out. Then she alternated this with a long-drawn-out: 'Daa-rling.'

Then there was night number two. The pink pantie went sailing out into the dark. There was a brief picture of Pelican-Beak sitting astride the face of Dan, then the gentleman dimmed the lights. This happened until all the panties were used up. She had dates as long as the panties lasted, then Dan remembered his role of God.

Pelican-Beak was too pushy for the new world. He began fixing her up. He broke her legs, he broke her jutting spindly elbows, he decorated her with tiny, pretty, pink roses for a new image of tender love. Out of her breasts, which were small, round and hard, he forced a black slime. Then he made her put on one of Elizabeth's bras. Her chest swelled up to Elizabeth's bust's size; she was supposed to have absorbed Elizabeth's harmless qualities by fitting her bra. Then he decided that the Pelican-Beak was too dangerous; she'd better quiet down totally. He'd re-design her pelvis area along the lines of Elizabeth's, which was extraordinarily passive and caused no trouble in the world. There, sure enough, at Elizabeth's side appeared a feminine pelvis with passive legs, nearly a replica of Elizabeth's. Poor Pelican-Beak had her own slashed off and was fitted out with the new pelvis. That job over, he dropped Pelican-Beak and turned to Miss Chopper.

Miss Chopper was a local lady with an insane passion for Dan. She walked around with a chopper slung over her shoulder. She threatened to behead all his women. Perhaps he just wanted Elizabeth to know how dangerous and un-attainable he really was, in case she got ideas and tried to make herself known to the living man. She had first to get past Miss Chopper. Indeed, all through this time he turned on two records. The one said:

'My darling, I have all these women, but I don't love them. If I lose you I have nothing else.'

The other record was a triumphant jeer:

'I am the king of sex. I go and go. I go with them all. They've been specially created for my desires. The road to me is past all those women. But need you try? You have nothing. I've shown you all they have, but you have nothing.'

There was a strange feeling in Elizabeth. The only two personalities who projected before her an overwhelming power were Medusa and Dan. There was a vastness about them, the personalities who accompanied their activities were extended replicas of their own selves. The sum total of it was a world where no one loved anyone. They were just barking savagely all the time; they were not human, or anything but permanently growling, hideous, savage beasts. She had no way of breaking the storm of evil – Dan was simply the extension of Medusa, and the torrent of hatred he felt for

Elizabeth was hitting her daily such terrible blows, she was barely alive. It was done under cover of the parade of the nice-time girls. As she lay down in the afternoon and slipped into a delirious collapse, a hosepipe squirting water would be thrust before her face. He'd hiss:

'Get up! Water your garden. You just lie here idle. You care about the poor, don't you?'

An anxiety about her work, which was failing day by day, would jerk her awake. As she'd try to rise from the bed, a heavy dead weight would press and press against her legs and body. It was extremely painful. His key aim seemed to be to allow her to have no rest at all. Nearly a year had passed by, sleepless. Towards the end of November, her endurance broke. Her mind was not functioning. In this state, he talked through her. They were hisses of hate. They were anything he pleased to say about people, anything he wished done. There was nothing in her to check the onrush of hell. And all the while the dirty little bastard moved around the village of Motabeng, grinning. Why, he and Sello had the performance of their lives. They operated the affairs of the universe in secret behind the scenes, but he, Dan, intended coming out top dog. The prophecies had to be smashed. He had brought Elizabeth to a state of breakdown. In just a little while he could smash the prophet image of Sello, through her.

The inclusion of old Mrs Jones in his plans was to widen the radius of scandal and sensation. He knew black people. They would run about and say to each other. 'Did you hear? She actually struck a white woman.' And, 'Did you hear what she said about *Sello?*'

Mrs Jones was one of the acquaintances Elizabeth had made through her gardening work. She was one of the oldest volunteers on the Motabeng project and had come over with her three daughters, all of whom were teachers. She was about fifty-five years old and had spent most of her life in a small English village. Her village had everything one usually read in the newspapers about England – the Left or Marxist revolutionaries, strikes, protests, spiritualists, nervous break-downs, dogs, vets and old men who donated their bodies to hospitals on their death. She had participated in everything

169

that was going on, and was very eager to communicate her long life history to Elizabeth. Like Tom, she became one of the regular callers at Elizabeth's house; but unlike Tom, with whom Elizabeth discussed the depth, breadth and height of the universe, Mrs Jones discussed nothing. Elizabeth was forced into the position of silent listener to the old woman's rambles. Mrs Jones's calls always began with:

'Elizabeth, I thought you might have some tomatoes. . . .'

She usually shuffled down the dusty brown road at about three and shuffled home at five. In between those times they had drunk tea (they both had a passion for tea) and Mrs Jones had fallen asleep several times during the recounting of her life-history. It must have been unconsciously boring to her as it was to Elizabeth. That was the key to her personality; her mental and emotional responses were those of a child; she interpreted life in the simplest terms. But children's chatter and behaviour is often interesting. Mrs Jones was child-like in an uninteresting way. She was full of platitudes after the style of Jesus Christ. She liked to say to Elizabeth:

'When people are lonely, I visit them. When people are sick, I visit them.'

She earnestly saw herself walking in the pathway of Christ, and tried to create imaginative situations in real life to fulfil all his sayings. Her life was so far removed from the stormy centre of Elizabeth's emotional life and thought that she was really like an innocent mouse building a nest near a slowly erupting volcano. The attractive thing about her, though, was that she was a replica of the humanity of the slum women Elizabeth had grown up with in South Africa. They had her motherly fussiness towards life, and her kindliness; they too had heard about Jesus and interpreted his statements in simple terms. Mrs Jones always had her short brown hair mussed up; she always looked sloppy. Anyone who lingered long enough in Elizabeth's company soon found out that she dealt with all the annoyances of life by rough, crude swear words. Bastard, damn and bloody hell were favourites. This fearfully titillated the old, pious church woman. She'd slap both hands on her knees, throw back her head and, with her mouth wide open, roar with laughter.

'Elizabeth,' she liked to say, confidingly. 'You'd never

believe I once belonged to the Left. It has changed since my young days. People have come to realize in England that Marxism is too materialistic. What happens after you have a TV in every room, a washing-machine and a deep-freeze? You aren't satisfied. I supported the working-class struggle. One gets very disillusioned with politics. It creates hate between people. I remember a time we used to stand on street corners in protest against the bomb, just silently you know, with our heads bent. . . .'

At this point she'd begin to doze, nodding and nodding her head until a particularly violent nod jerked her wide awake again. She'd look at Elizabeth, slap her hands on her knees, throw back her head and roar with laughter. But the history of her own life intrigued her. She started it every other afternoon: 'You'd never believe I once belonged to the Left . . .' and fell asleep at 'our heads bent. . . .'

She was still rambling on like this when Dan silently stole the show from her. The innocent, kindly, boring old woman died a dramatic death before Elizabeth's eyes. He turned on his hiss record. She's not all she seems to be on the surface, it said. Since he was God, he had top-secret information about her soul-history. Even prostitutes had to have mothers. She was the origin of his nice-time girls. Her symbol was that of a broody hen sitting on a clutch of bad eggs. Like Sello, she rose on the horizon like a monstrous, cackling old witch. Between September and November Elizabeth had enough physical stamina to reel in and out of her nightmare; but the propaganda records, the repetitive images of evil, about Sello, about old Mrs Jones, about women, children, men, animals, about all life shattered her sanity into a thousand fragments. The day she broke down she simply howled, and like a volcano the evil erupted in a wild flow of molten lava.

Late November that year they closed the local-industries project. There was a promise of rain in the air; heavy black storm-clouds swept across the wide arc of Motabeng sky. Some members had lands they wanted to prepare for ploughing, and this disrupted group work. It was decided to close temporarily, till ploughing was through. But the garden group, who had no lands, were to have no holiday; vegetables were full-time work. Elizabeth stumbled out of the meeting. Kenosi silently padded after her a little of the way. She turned on her and hissed fiercely: 'I am ill', and she reeled slowly homewards with the last ounce of her strength.

Kenosi, out of habit, walked down to Elizabeth's home the following morning. Elizabeth kept the seed of the garden, as they had as yet no storage shed. She stopped at the gate and stared at the closed front door and drawn curtains. After five minutes of silent indecision, she turned and walked back up the dusty brown road, and down the valley to the garden. They were never to see each other till seven months later when Elizabeth came out of hospital. Unfortunately for her, Mrs Jones lived by her platitudes. She did not have the wariness of Kenosi, who scented uncommon happenings behind that closed door. Kenosi reported to Eugene. Eugene muttered to a teacher that Elizabeth was ill. Two days later Mrs Jones came shuffling down the road: 'When people are lonely, I visit them. When people are sick, I visit them. . . .'

She knocked loudly at Elizabeth's door. Elizabeth opened the door, then stood blocking her entry, a terrible cumulus cloud of hate. She wasn't seeing old Mrs Jones but the cackling witch of her nightmare, the mother of the nice-time girls.

'Elizabeth,' Mrs Jones said, screwing up her face anxiously, 'I heard you were ill and came to visit you.'

Elizabeth did not reply. They hung on each other like that, the old woman barely escaping her death. She seemed not to feel the explosion. She reached out one hand and touched Elizabeth, brought her face quite close, and said in a confidential whisper:

'I'm going to pray for you.'

'It depends on which God you're praying to,' Elizabeth said violently and slammed the door.

That was about ten o'clock in the morning. She turned from the door, swayed to the sink for a glass of water, drank it and immediately threw it up on the floor. She had not eaten anything for two days. She had lost track of the small boy. She could not communicate with him in any way. He crawled in and out of the house. He had friends. He had eaten somewhere. He was so cunning about his own survival that she only saw him at sunset when he came home to bed.

She swayed to the bed and collapsed. The whole room, her whole head was full of shifting ghostly shapes and images. It was Dan's seventy-one nice-time girls. They crawled over her in a slow death-dance. Hands moved, grabbing for the last treasures in the debris of her shattered life.

Sello was there with a boy-friend. His swollen, lopsided, greenish-hued face grinned at her evilly. His little girl still lay with her face upturned in death. The cackling Mrs Jones egged her offspring on to take everything while the going was good. Dan might have been the only presence there. A terrible weight was exterminating her. In her ears was a low, wild, panting hysteria:

'Die, die, die, you dog! I hate you! I hate you!'

Her mind struggled with the question: 'Why, why, why? What have I done?'

She struck an abyss of utter darkness, where all appeals for mercy, relief, help were simply a mockery. At what point did she come to the terrible decision – 'I'll die, but I'll take one of them along with me!' Because it was already pitch-dark when she stood up in her nightdress and ran out of the house. Sello and Dan lived at the extreme end of Motabeng village, twenty miles away, but the home of Mrs Jones was just a few yards from her own house. She ran up the brown road and turned in at the school gates. Old Mrs Jones had been out visiting a friend. She had a torch in her hand, and as she approached the gate of her house the light of the torch struck against the form of Elizabeth.

'Elizabeth!' she cried out.

An angry roar greeted her. Elizabeth rushed towards her.

'Don't you know?' she shouted, 'oh, don't you know? You make your children prostitutes!'

She raised one hand and struck the old woman a blow on the side of the head. Mrs Jones cringed. The torch dropped to the ground. They stood a moment, silent, breathless in the dark; then Elizabeth turned her face up to the stars and screamed. Hard, running footsteps came from all directions towards them in the dark. Someone grabbed hold of Elizabeth's arm, shook her and shouted: 'What's wrong? What's wrong?'

She tore her arm free and began running. The footsteps pursued her. She stopped, turned round and swore violently. The pursuers fell back. She ran, she screamed, she ran until she reached her home and locked the door. The footsteps, the anxious whispers stopped at the gate. She heard them.

'What shall we do? What shall we do?' they said.

Like Kenosi, they stared in silent indecision at the house and retreated. Elizabeth turned to the small boy. She was trembling from head to toe.

'I'll kill him first, then I'll kill myself,' she thought.

He was already in bed. He sat up and looked at her, then quite calmly pushed back the blankets, stood up, and walked towards her.

'What's wrong?' he asked. 'Why was you screaming?'

'I beat Mrs Jones,' she said.

He laughed a bit, either through nerves or because the idea of it was grotesquely funny. Then he bent his head and walked with quiet determined footsteps to her bed, sat on the edge of it and pressed his hands together in his lap. He looked up at her with the manly air of one who is about to settle all the nonsense in the household.

'Why was you talking to yourself in the night?' he asked, pointedly. 'You talk all the time, then you shout: Leave me! Leave me! I get frightened. I cover my head.'

She stared back at him in appalled silence. So that was what it had come to? She knew about the silent soliloquies of that year of sleepless nights, but she wasn't aware that she had begun talking them out loud.

'It's nothing, my darling,' she said, anxiously. 'Some people are bothering me. I'll chase them away.'

He looked up at her trustingly. For all her haphazard ways and unpredictable temperament, she was the only authority he had in his life. The trust he showed, the way he quietly walked back to his own bed, feverishly swerved her mind away from killing him, then herself. But death was there. In the swirling turmoil of her mind she clutched at Sello. All night long she sat up, planning his death. She saw her own doom, but a violent rage within insisted on another victim. She quite forgot that the child could overhear. She started pacing up and down muttering to herself:

'That's the sum total of them, he and Dan. They're operating only from the bottom. Why must they choke the life out of me? So few shreds of my sanity remain.' She paused, turned to the room where Sello, the monk, sat and shouted: 'I'm not the dog of the Africans, do you hear? I'm not the dog of these bloody bastard Batswana, do you hear? It's you, you and Dan, you are so weak you don't care where you put your penis. Why must I be the audience of *shit*? Huh? I sleep with cows. I sleep with men. I sleep with my daughter. I sleep with dogs. I sleep with pigs. That's all you want to do, sleep with cows and pigs and dogs and God knows what. What's wrong with you, Sello? Why must you alternate lives of sainthood with spells of debauchery? Why do you show me two worlds – the saints who died in prison and the dolls and prostitutes with Mary Magdalene in the lead? Do you think you're having the biggest joke of all time – ha, ha, ha, I'm Jesus and the devil too? What did you say to me? We made the soul straight, the truths of the universe were dominant – then after all those philosophies of yours, what's going on here? Why are you secretly destroying me?'

She asked all these questions, but was beyond hearing any reply. Who would have answered? Sello had maintained a deathly silence for a year. Dan kept on revolving his penis in her face. There was no escape from Dan. There was no escape from the satanic image of Sello, his boy-friend, his little girl with her face upturned in death. The stage remained set. Her screaming, agonized nervous system snapped to pieces. By dawn, at about four-thirty, she got on her bicycle and took a mad ride, five miles to the central part of Motabeng village. She had a scrawled note in her pocket:

'SELLO IS A FILTHY PERVERT WHO SLEEPS WITH HIS DAUGHTER.'

She signed her name and surname under it and stuck it up on the wall of Motabeng post office. She cycled back home dead to the vibrant beauty of the early morning which she loved so much; dead to everything, recklessly inviting her own death.

By eight that morning a police van drew up outside her house. Two Batswana police stepped out, opened the gate and walked up the pathway to her door. As she answered the knock on the door, one of the men showed her the paper she had stuck on the post office.

'You're Elizabeth, aren't you?' he asked. 'Did you write this?'

'Yes,' she said.

'We'd like to come in,' he said.

She moved to one side, then they waited until she was seated opposite them. The small boy had just woken up. It was school holidays. He sat bolt upright, looking at the police with huge, staring eyes.

'Why did you write this?' the same man queried.

She could not think of any explanation other than the incoherence she lived with. She said: 'You must know of these prophecies about Sello. I did it because he's God and the devil at the same time.'

He kept quiet and stared back at her, expressionlessly. Then he said: 'We thought you might be ill, and arranged for you to be admitted to hospital. We'll take you there now.'

'What will happen to my child?' she asked.

'People never live alone in the world,' he said, easily. 'You have friends here. We'll find them and they will look after the child.'

He stood up and took the small boy by the hand. She followed.

It was the same hospital bed, the same private ward she had been in nearly a year and a half ago. A doctor sat on the side of her bed.

'What's wrong?' he asked, kindly.

She looked back at him. She could only give him the incoherent statement she had made to the police.

'Please help me,' she said. 'It's Sello. He's both God and the devil at the same time.'

He reached out and touched her hand.

'Don't worry about that,' he said. 'We'll sedate you for about a week, then you'll feel better.' He turned to a nurse standing by his side with a tray. 'Give her a shot every three hours.'

The nurse smiled at her. She had a sleep-drug in the syringe: 'Turn over,' she said.

Almost eagerly Elizabeth turned and exposed her thigh. It had been months and months since she had last slept. Nothing, not even heavy doses of sleeping-tablets, could shut out the feverish nightmare of Dan. She barely felt the prick of the needle. She began skidding, swirling, reeling into oblivion. A face flared up briefly in the billowing darkness. His face was flung back like Christ crucified.

'Oh, what have you done?' he said, anguished. 'They'd told me. It couldn't possibly be true.'

Then she blanked out totally.

It must have been for about three hours she lay like that, because shortly after she awoke a nurse came in with a tray of food and another injection. She lay staring at the patch of blue sky outside, long slow tears rolling helplessly out of her eyes. Al Capone had pressed the button to the boys downstairs. They were mixing the cement. She hadn't seen Dan's form just then, but shortly before she awoke she had seen two large, familiar black hands move towards her head. They had opened her skull. He'd bent his mouth towards the cavity and talked right into the exposed area. His harsh, grating voice was unintelligible. It just said: 'Rrrrrrrrraaaaaaaaa.' It had shot through her body with the pain of knife wounds. She'd pulled and pulled, struggling to free herself of the hands holding her head. She'd awoken gasping for breath.

The nurse was friendly. She saw the tears.

'Are you worried about your son?' she asked. 'You must not worry. When people are sick someone will always help. The teachers at Motabeng Secondary love you very much. We've been answering phone calls about you the whole morning. Mrs Stanley is taking care of your son. She is coming at four o'clock to see you. She says she will bring the child with her, so I'll give you your injection after visiting-time. Eat your food now.'

Elizabeth moved to sit up. Her head exploded with pain.

'Do you have any Aspro?' she asked. 'I have a terrible headache.'

The nurse nodded, walked out briskly and returned with

a glass of water and two Aspro. Then she nodded and smiled again and walked out, closing the door.

A little while later Mrs Stanley walked in with her son. She was middle-aged, friendly in an eager bird-like way with a round dumpy motherly figure.

'We'd be so happy to have Shorty till you are better, Elizabeth,' she said. 'All our little ones are grown up and away, and I told Peter it would be great fun having a little one in the house again. We're going away on holiday in a few days and taking him with us.'

They'd become friends over the vegetable garden. Mrs Jones, who was also a friend of Mrs Stanley, had passed on the information that Elizabeth was particularly fond of tea, so whenever Elizabeth walked into Mrs Stanley's house with cabbages and tomatoes she immediately put on the kettle for tea. How had she built up such patterns of affection in the horrific clamour of her life, and what could she say about assaulting Mrs Jones? She said the wrong thing.

'Mrs Jones thinks she knows everything about God,' Elizabeth said, defensively.

Mrs Stanley stared back at her steadily and did not reply. The small boy touched her hand.

'Mrs Stanley gave me some money,' he said. 'I bought you a sucker and a ballpoint pen because you like to write.'

Mrs Stanley smiled down at him, affectionately. He was still fiddling in his pockets. He took out about a dozen suckers.

'Where are you going to hide these suckers for me?' he asked. 'I can take four of them for my best friends, but you was saying I mustn't eat all the sweets on one day.'

Mrs Stanley bent down and took the suckers out of his hands.

'It's all right, Shorty,' she said. 'I'll hide them for you.'

He carefully counted out four suckers and handed the rest to her. She put them into her handbag.

'If I die. . .' Elizabeth began morbidly.

Mrs Stanley went red in the face and tears shot into her eyes.

'Lots of people have nervous breakdowns,' she said. 'They get over it.'

'What if it's not really a breakdown, but a planned death one cannot escape?'

Again Mrs Stanley kept silent and stared back at Elizabeth.

'I'm not afraid of physical death,' Elizabeth persisted. 'But I am afraid of a soul death. There's no God where I am now.'

Mrs Stanley bent her head: 'I'm sorry,' she said.

The small boy, who had been listening to this, said in careful imitation of Mrs Stanley: 'I'm sorry.'

The two women burst out laughing, but Shorty had something to say about death. It had finally caught up with him.

'I saw a dog what died,' he said, earnestly. 'It was lying on one side with a big hole in its stomach. I don't like to die.'

Mrs Stanley took his hand: 'Come on, Shorty,' she said. 'No one is going to die. You are going to an orange farm with me, and you're going to stuff yourself with oranges. There's a river there too, where you can catch fish.'

He turned his face towards her, bewitched. He knew what to do with such wonders and things. The adorable woman turned to Elizabeth, waved goodbye and walked out clutching the small boy by the hand. There was nothing else for Elizabeth to do but continue the war with hell. Mercifully, Shorty had been pulled out of it.

It seemed too fantastic to recall what happened to her between that time and the time she came out of hospital. It seemed like the typical record of a lunatic, except that a part of her mind kept clear, silently observing all that was done to her by Dan. The other part was so chaotic and panic-stricken that words, jumbled sentences she uttered, threw her straight into the loony bin a week later. They'd just given her another injection at sunset. She lay staring at the dusky mauve patch of sunset sky, not quite sure at what point she dozed off. Dan's hand moved towards her head again. He held in his hand the broken-off end of a bottle. He lifted it and bashed it again and again into her head with a wild frenzy. She opened dead eyes and stared at the darkness. Not anything was alive in her, except her body. This they transferred to a mental hospital some six hundred miles from Motabeng.

The doctor of the Motabeng hospital had come around

the next morning and sat at her bedside with a notebook.

'Could you give me some idea of what is troubling you?' he'd asked.

'Sello,' she whispered.

She could not get beyond that. Logically, a story had a beginning. She was being killed by Dan, but Sello had started it. The story had begun with Sello and Medusa. He sat a little while, taking down some notes. She had no clear idea of what she was saying. She was struggling to recapture the image of Medusa and what Medusa and Sello had done to her, and she couldn't get it straight. After a time he closed his book, turned to her and said:

'I'm not a psychiatrist. I can't treat mental breakdowns. I'll have to transfer you to a mental hospital. But you just rest here while I make the arrangements.'

'I don't want any more of those injections,' she said, feebly.

'Why not?' he asked.

'They suffocate me. I can't breathe.' She really meant she did not want to fall asleep. Dan was bashing in her head the moment she blacked out. He was right there beside her bed, wild, excited into a frenzy at her helplessness. He hacked her to death between blackouts. She had no defence. She simply lay there falling into death. The joy and ecstasy for him was the piecemeal job he was doing. He left a little part of her alive each time. It was most probably his major sexual erection; he attacked her head the way he had attacked the vaginas of the nice-time girls he'd displayed before her for a whole year. He had a way of conveying hideous, silent, concealed laughter through monstrous images of women being raped. No thought against him could shape itself in her mind. He turned up his propaganda records when he pleased:

'My darling, if I lose you I have nothing else,' they churned on monotonously.

It was a Saturday morning when she arrived at the loony bin. The attendants there greeted lunatics with laughter. She was a big surprise. It was strictly for poor, illiterate Batswana, who were treated like animals. They seemed to be the only people who went insane in Botswana, and because they were poor and illiterate and it was a government hospital they were provided with no soap for bathing or towels to dry the body. The place had a terrible stench.

The attendants took away her clothes and handed her a brown cotton dress. She had no underwear. She stood for a moment gazing dismally around the stinking hospital ward, then turned and lay down on a bed. One of the nurses approached her, grinning.

'I hear you have a child,' she said.

Elizabeth flew into a violent rage: 'Do you care a damn?' she shouted. 'Leave me alone.'

The nurse grinned. Loony-bin case confirmed. They were all like that. Later Elizabeth said to Tom she didn't know how she got out of there, but on looking back a strange comedy of errors built up around her. She knew what was happening to her. She knew her murderer. She knew he was viciously, savagely, wildly, dangerously evil, but he was top dog. He was revelling in the power of life and death he had over her, something like the way the cat bashes the mouse around, slowly, patiently. In that sense, she bowed down. But the clear part of her mind. was saying: 'You bloody, damn, stinking, filthy bastard. Oh, you bloody, dirty, filthy bastard.'

She turned around and said this to the Batswana nurses. They said: 'Look here, this isn't a hospital where patients lie down. You must get up and help to clean up the place. The patients work here.'

Indeed they did. The patients washed out the whole ward in the early morning, swept the grounds, washed the linen; the attendants stood around supervising. In any case, Elizabeth had no legs to stand on; she was just a walking corpse, but on being told this she shouted back: 'I'm not an African. Don't you see? I never want to be an African. You bloody well, damn well leave me alone!'

They did. They believed her.

She said much the same thing to the doctor on the Monday morning she first saw him. She said she had nothing to say and simply wanted to be left alone. He flared up. He was terribly important because he was the only psychiatrist the country had. All the literate, expensive patients he had! The way the country couldn't bear to lose him. The way he knew his job, he said, and who was she to refuse treatment? She stared back at him, haughtily. He was just a semi-literate quack doctor from Europe.

'Go!' he said. 'I don't care whether you stay here for three years.'

Apart from giving her sedatives three times a day, everyone ignored her. She settled down to her own routine; she lay all day long staring through a window at a hillside on which trees grew, and watched the movement of the sun from sunrise till it set behind the hill. The small boy always came walking down the dusty brown road at sunset, lost in his playtime thoughts. A letter came from Mrs Stanley, with a box of chocolates and a small note from her son. He spelt 'dear' wrong: 'Dare Mother, when are you coming home?' She only cried silently. It was just a matter of waiting for death. In moments of deep depression she contemplated suicide, and started to collect the sedatives so as to swallow about sixty, one day.

One day a nurse approached her and said: 'You must get up. You have a visitor.'

'Who?' she asked.

'He's a white man. He says his name is Tom. He says he is your friend.'

She sat up a little and said sharply: 'Tell him I don't want to see him.'

The nurse laughed: 'Yo!' she said. 'You *are* mad, aren't you? You hate black people. You hate white people. You hate everyone.'

But she walked out to deliver the message. Soon she returned and said: 'He refuses to go. He says he must see you. He says he can bring you anything you need. He says he is your friend.'

Suddenly getting rid of Tom seemed to be a life-and-death issue to her. With a trembling hand, she searched in her locker for the ballpoint pen given her by her son, dug up a piece of paper and wrote: 'Tom, I never ever want to see you again, now or for the rest of eternity.'

The nurse went out with the letter and returned with a parcel which she placed on Elizabeth's locker. It was a carton of cigarettes.

'You are bad,' she commented crossly. 'He read your letter and started to cry. Here's his letter.'

'I'll see you again, Elizabeth,' it said, defiantly.

She pushed her face into the pillow and howled. Immediately the nurse was all tender sympathy. She rubbed Elizabeth's hand softly and said: 'Everybody understands the ways of sick people. Don't cry now.' Then she bent and whispered conspiratorially in Elizabeth's ear: 'Perhaps he's your boy-friend?'

Elizabeth burst out laughing: 'I'm as old as his mother. He's my son. He hates me to say that, because he's the manly type. They don't have mothers.'

'Yo!' she said, laughing too. 'So you're a human being? We are calling you wild animal because you're always so angry.'

Elizabeth stared into the distance: 'I'm only angry about one thing,' she said.

'What?'

'Sello,' she said.

She looked at the nurse and asked: 'You know Sello?'

The nurse shook her head: 'The doctor told us not to allow you to talk about Sello.'

What sparked off the comedy of errors was the way the internal torture kept shooting out of her. She'd fly into a rage and start shouting about not being an African. Dan won her her liberation from the loony bin. She meant him. She meant she hated those black hands that were bashing her head to pieces. She meant that if she could get hold of him she'd gouge out his eyes, she'd tear him to pieces. She expressed this to innocent people. One day she sprang off the bed, stamped her feet hard on the floor and let out a stream of abuse at the nurse. She ran to report her to the doctor; returned, and said coldly:

'Doctor wants to see you.'

To Elizabeth's surprise he was smiling genially. He waved one hand expansively in the air and said: 'Have a seat. Would you like some tea?'

She nodded her head. He poured the tea and lowering his voice said: 'These people are *bad*. They are *liars*.'

A wild alarm-bell sounded off inside her. He pushed the

cup of tea towards her as though she were an old friend. She had to fight an impulse to jump up and run out of his office. He was stark raving mad too. He really hated black people. There was no way she could even begin to discuss her nightmare with him. He let fly about the country. It was full of South African spies. They needn't think they could do a thing with *their* independence. The country was really run by the South African government. That was the beginning of his assumed friendship with her. Before that day, he could not stand the sight of her because she had insulted his profession. It dawned on her further that this was the road out of the loony bin. He assured her that she was not really ill. She only had a slight nervous breakdown. She kept deathly silent, flaming with humiliation and guilt. The only good thing it did was to put an end to her abuse of the nurses. After that she walked around silently, apologetically. She got out of bed, helped to sweep the yard and took an interest in her surroundings. The shock of being thought of as a comrade racialist had abruptly restored a portion of her sanity. But she made no effort to convince him they were not on the same track.

'Ah,' said the doctor. 'You are better already. You are helping. You set the table for lunch. You will soon go home. You are cured. You have a little boy? How old is he?'

She turned to him eagerly. It was Shorty's birthday in a few weeks' time.

'Could I send some money to Mrs Stanley for his birthday?' she asked. 'He'll be seven years old.'

'Of course, of course,' he said expansively. 'I'll help you with the cheque.'

That was the really beautiful thing about him – he loved children. Neither did his racialism extend to a black man who was also the father of children. He turned to her and said:

'I don't like what you said about the man, Sello. It was *bad*.' And he looked away sadly into the distance.

At the time she had only stared back at him, unmoved; but later, when it dawned on her that Dan was a living, vicious, total untruth, that he'd propelled her through pressure of torture into that false statement about Sello, she nearly died.

The doctor told her that he had eight children. In case she did not believe him, he brought them all to the hospital one Saturday morning and introduced them to her. The eldest girl had long brown hair that fell way down her back. He was so proud of the children, he beamed expansively and said: 'You see, Elizabeth. You'll soon be seeing your own son.'

Apart from the sedatives and conversations about her son, he never bothered to probe the causes of her breakdown. He might have been a quack doctor and a racialist, but he was also a magnificent human being with a kind heart. A few weeks after Shorty's birthday, she returned home.

She hardly recognized Shorty. Mrs Stanley had let him gallivant wherever he liked, and he had turned into Huckleberry Finn! He and a small friend, Oliver, had bravely set out one day to find the edge of the world. They wanted to see all the goats falling off, he said. Then he looked at her accusingly. Oliver's father had found them lost and wandering in the bush. He'd told them there was no such thing as the edge of the world. In fact, Shorty was thoroughly disgruntled at the idea of being her son, because he had had such a whale of a time with Mrs Stanley.

'You can't cook like Mrs Stanley,' he moaned. 'I ate whatever I liked. If I wanted anything she gave it me. You always say no, no, no.'

Then he looked at her with dark eyes and said:

'All the standard two's are saying you are mad.'

She had just arrived home. She was still desperately ill. She had only strained her nerves to get out of the loony bin because the conditions were so terrible. She half propped herself up on the bed and said, irritably:

'Of course I'm mad. If you don't want to stay in this house you can take your blessed things and clear out. A lot of people want children.'

He looked at her a little apprehensively from his position on the floor mat beside the bed. She had a terrible way of matching words to deeds, and he hadn't meant things to go *that* far. He adopted a softer tone.

'I like mothers,' he said, cunningly.

He fidgeted. The afternoon sun was calling him out to play. The whole morning had gone by in lessons at school. He liked playtime best.

'I have a football team,' he said. 'I know how to play football. Will you buy me a football?'

'Yes,' she said.

'When?' he asked.

'Tomorrow,' she said.

He stood up, quivering with joy, and shot out of the house, not to be seen again till sunset. There was a whole afternoon ahead of her of depression and pointless thinking. She couldn't seem to live without some kind of drug; the screaming tension of her nerves was intensely painful. Along the way home she had bought a few bottles of beer. It never really helped. The beer only carried her down to the deepest pit of depression and she sat there numbed, unthinking. She had just begun to sip the beer when, very clearly, Sello said: 'Hello.'

She paused, propped herself up on one arm and looked towards the room where Sello sat.

'Are you still sitting in my house, Sello?' she said, loudly. 'What do you want from me now? I'm dead. There's no more entertainment for you. Why don't you go away?'

'I stay here because I like you,' he said.

'Agh,' she said. 'I go to the loony bin. There's hell. I come back. There's hell. Where does it all end?'

From a corner of her bedroom Dan sprang vividly alive.

'You are going to end it,' he said. 'You are going to commit suicide.'

She kept silent. She had enough drugs on her to do it. She was depressed enough to end her life.

'It's over,' he said wildly. 'It's over.'

Ha, ha, ha. Her great romance with the super-slick Casanova was through. He'd declared it. But there were terms. The bloody bastard switched off one record only to turn on another:

'Suffer from unrequited love for me.' A racking pain filled her chest.

It took her a few days to realize what was happening. The

drama was speeding to a close. The two men were conducting, in different ways, a fierce struggle over her nearly dead body. Sello was pressuring her back into life. Death had the coffin. He was screwing in the nails. That afternoon he dramatically produced the day and time of death. It was the following day at a quarter to one. He followed this announcement by a terror threat.

'There's no point in your staying alive,' he said. 'You've no self-control left. The only road for you is prostitution. You are going to have eight affairs.' And he moved his splaying hands loosely from side to side.

Numbly, she dozed, her head spinning with beer and drugs. Just at sunset there was a familiar shout at the gate:

'Elizabeth! Here I am!'

She sprang to her feet and rushed to the door. 'Tom!' she shouted.

In a second life swirled around her. The heavy boots twinkled up the pathway. He paused at the door, beaming.

'I'd just heard you were back and came rushing over,' he said.

She burst out laughing.

'After all I've said to you?' she said.

He swung into the house.

'You can call me any damn thing you like – bastard, member of the Ku Klux Klan – I don't care,' he said.

She gasped: 'Did I really say that, Tom?'

'Of course you did,' he said. He turned and mimicked the high, shrill hysteria of her voice: 'Tom, do you think you can escape the taint of the Ku Klux Klan? You're tainted with it too. You're all bastards.' Then he laughed as though this were the most delightful thing she had ever said to him.

'I'm sorry,' she said.

He continued laughing. He put a parcel down on the edge of the sink, stripped off a soiled sweater and, as usual, started to wash.

'God,' he said, teasingly. 'When you raise hell, you raise hell. Lucrezia Borgia, where did you get all that thunder from?'

He threw back his head and laughed, gloriously.

'You scared hell out of that daft old bird, Jones,' he said.

'You know what she ran around saying? "Elizabeth hates me. It's impossible. I'm going to show you all that love overcomes hatred." She's stone daft.'

'I'm sorry,' Elizabeth said, stricken. She saw her own death right in front of her. 'What do you have here, Tom?' she said, distractedly touching the parcels.

'It's food,' he said. 'Kidneys, rice, lettuce, tomatoes. I thought you couldn't have any food in the house so I brought along some for supper.'

She moved to take a pot from under the sink to prepare the food.

'Leave it!' he commanded. 'I'll cook. You go and sit down. You look just like death.'

She moved and sat down on her son's couch bed. Sello, who was sitting on the chair just in front of her, moved sharply into focus. He turned the intangible outline of his face towards her and said: 'I love him.'

'I love him too,' she said.

'What did you say?' Tom asked from the kitchen, clattering with the pots for rice and kidney stew.

'I said I love you,' she said.

He put down the pot and came and sat beside her and flung one arm behind her neck.

'Lucrezia Borgia,' he said, tenderly. 'Don't you love everyone? Remember what you said to me that day we first met in the vegetable garden? You said that if the garden had a big street down the middle with lots of side-streets people could come and look around at everything. You said you thought the vegetables would like it too. And I thought to myself: "What do we have here — fish or fowl? This is one hell of a girl. Ha, ha, ha, how does she know what vegetables like?" Isn't that love, not only for people but vegetables too?'

Her soul-death was really over in that instant, though she did not realize it. He seemed to have, in an intangible way, seen her sitting inside that coffin, reached down and pulled her out. The rest she did herself. She was poised from that moment to make the great leap out of hell.

'You know Sello . . .' she began.

'Don't worry about that,' he said. 'Eugene was so worried,

he phoned him. Sello said: "It's obvious she's been living under some terrible strain, isn't it?" He didn't take it seriously.'

'I did it because I thought I hated him for valid reasons,' she said.

'You are quite wrong,' he said, seriously. 'People were shocked and upset for his sake. He swayed all the sympathy in your direction. He said the right things and remained undisturbed. He's a great man.'

She kept quiet and stared at Sello sitting in front of her It was his own fault. He liked lunatic situations like this, he liked to travel about in the air with his soul. It was preferable to behave in an ordinary way, not like what was going on in her life.

'There's things I want to tell you, Tom, about Sello, about hell,' she said. 'I need to talk to someone, because there's a terrible pain inside.'

'All right,' he said, jumping up. 'Let me prepare the food first.'

As he moved around he continued talking.

'Are you going down to the garden?'

'Yes,' she said.

'When?'

'I don't know, Tom. I don't feel well.'

'You'll be all right soon. You'll find a day when everything looks fine. You needn't care a damn about what people think. They forget. In a month or two it's all forgotten, though there's a lot of whispering just now.'

'I wasn't faced with the normal,' she said, despairingly.

'I could see,' he said. 'There was a hell of a war going on.'

'Tom,' she said. 'You'll come around till I can stand on my feet?'

'Of course,' he said. 'I'll be here every day.'

The odour of frying kidneys filled the house. He sliced up the salad and tomatoes into a bowl. Shorty opened the door and crept into the house. They were both hungry after their outdoor chores. As soon as Tom set the food on the table, they began to eat ravenously, casting longing glances at Elizabeth's untouched plate. She slowly sipped a bottle of beer. At the right moment she pushed her plate to the centre of the table. The two hungry wolves pounced on it, sharing it between them. She stared at them from a great distance. They glowed with energy and life, untouched by the crater-like wreckage of her life. Tom gathered all the plates together to wash them in the sink.

'Elizabeth,' he said, joyously. 'I like your house. You never seem to have any washing up to do. When I eat at other houses the washing up takes me hours. They just have piles of dirty dishes in the sink.'

Shorty washed himself in the bathroom. Tom slowly sipped a beer. He turned his face towards her with that special, ancient, wise-man expression she loved so much.

'What did you want to tell me?' he asked.

It seemed hours went by with her broken, disjointed talk.

'You'd never think of it like that, Tom, would you?' she said. 'I've lost my sense of goodness completely; just the ordinary kind people use from day to day. I've seen a form of greed and grabbing and an arrogance monstrously out of proportion to normal human feelings. The first thing I've always done is to act on wild impulse. My temperament was unequal to what I've lived through for three years or more. I seem to have taken a strange journey into hell and darkness. I could not grasp the darkness because at the same time I saw the light. That captured and riveted my attention. It was Sello. It seemed to me that his job was religion itself, because he moved towards me like that, then right in front of my eyes did a slow, spiritual strip-tease act. He half showed me that the source of human suffering was God itself, personalities in possession of powers or energies of the soul. Ordinary people never mucked up the universe. They don't have that kind of power, wild and flaring out of proportion. They have been the victims of it. . . .'

He almost sprang out of his chair.

'Wait a bit. You have something there. I want to hold that thought a while,' he said.

He sat for a while brooding deeply, fitting her words into his own mental pattern. He was really a brilliant thinker. She always depended on him to add to her own thoughts. After a while he nodded for her to go on.

She continued: 'Sello briefly showed me a time far back

when these personalities had insight into their powers. Then human life was simply an expendable commodity. Their powers deluded them into a sense of supremacy at the expense of other human lives. He seemed to have held total sway of the situation as Old Father Time. He sent the destiny of mankind crashing down into darkness. His exact words were: "I am the root cause of human suffering." It seemed like everyone was rubbing their nose in the dirt at that time. The dirt lingered like a dark stream through human destiny. Again he assumed total sway, and turned the whole destiny of man towards the light. I say this because his voice still lingers as the dominant theme of human morality. He re-created the image of godliness or goodness. The powers and energies were still there, but this time he produced personalities like Buddha. Buddha moved slowly towards me so I got a good look at his face. His eyelids covered his eyes. His whole life had been turned inwards. It was not that of a prancing power-maniac concentrating on earthly thrones and prestige. The holiness of soul he had was even indifferent to prayers or anything. He heard nothing. He cared about nothing. He had become nothing but his inward simplicity. To face that and at the same time face African destiny, African circumstances, was like signing my own death-warrant in advance. The brutality of my experience here has been so terrible, the things done to me so degrading – God knows how I am still alive! And it isn't only Sello. . . .'

She looked at him helplessly. She did not know what to say about Dan. He was indescribable. She returned to Sello as the thread of coherence.

'Sello made me believe that mankind basically had now acquired the soul-pattern I saw on the face of Buddha. Lots of people looked like him in their souls. I was so exalted those days I simply took a wild mental leap. I thought: Mankind will awaken to the wonder in their own souls. Poverty will be solved overnight; there are so many magnificent people alive. It didn't work out like that. I ended up in the loony bin and I'm nearly dead. . . .'

'You're wrong about one thing,' he said, seriously. 'You're wrong about this mankind waking up business. I hope they never do. I don't trust them. Once they see something they'll use it to kill each other. Everything that could be useful, like atomic energy, they use for death. If they get an idea that they have inner powers too, can you imagine what they'd do?'

She nodded. That was just where she was. Wasn't Dan a magnificent display of inner power, and what did he do with it? 'When I go I go on for one hour. Die, you dog, there's no place for you.'

'I've resolved nothing,' she said, miserably. 'Things I'd never have thought of get to dominate my mind and create neurotic fears. I'd never have thought twice of what Jesus said. He said the soul was really open territory easily invaded by devils. They just move in, carry on, mess around, and when a man has cleaned up his house, ten thousand more move in. If I had to take up residence in somebody's house I'd be polite and enquire after their health. Devils don't do that. They just walk in and smash everything up and then they grin. . . .'

'Why don't you find a husband, Elizabeth?' he asked. 'It would be a defence. You're attacked because you are too alone.'

'It's not a part of my calculations, Tom,' she said. 'I seem to have been born for this experience. I had tremendous stamina. Someone weighed up my soul and set the seal of doom on it. I'm opposing him because I think I ought to live too, like everyone else. I don't care to be shoved out of the scheme of things. I want to live the way I am without anyone dictating to me. Maybe in some other life I'll just be a woman cooking food and having babies, but just now Shylock is demanding his pound of flesh. I have to attend the trial. . . .'

He was so busy. He was working against time. She couldn't last long, and he had a masterpiece of his own to produce. He'd been present when Sello had said to her:

'Then we said: Send us perfection. They sent you. Then we asked: What is perfection? And they said: Love.'

Dan had to outdo Sello in everything. He was producing its opposite. She could see him wiping up the legs a bit because they were too dirty. Then supposedly, since he was God, he breathed into it the breath of life. The model stood up and turned to face Elizabeth. They were identical replicas except that what stood before Elizabeth was a demon of sensuousness. She had thick, swollen, sensual lips. She rolled her eyes with a mock innocence. Her legs were so weak she could hardly stand on them. She oozed horror and slime. Dan did not waste his energies on imagery. He had spent a year giving Elizabeth unsought inside information on sex. The result of this lengthy training was the model in front of her. He behaved as though he had his own programme for the future – a ball of wild revelry and evil. He had bent and broken her soul to fit in with this future. It was not in him to ask people's likes and dislikes – after all, didn't they say: man proposes but God disposes? If he'd a plan, and he was God, everyone had to fit in with it, even if they did not care to be prostitutes.

Then Dan moved towards her. There wasn't any need for her existence any longer. His hands reached for her head. He'd been doing this for months, opening her skull and talking into it in a harsh, grating voice. When she opened her eyes a few hours later her mind was a total blank. She could not remember who she was, where she was, what day it was. There was nothing in her head. Was this his way of showing her how near the end was?

Shorty stood up and padded on bare feet to her bed. She couldn't remember his name. The cunning little bugger wanted his football. He smiled sweetly and rubbed her cheek. She was afraid to ask: 'Who are you?'

'You won't forget my football, mother?' he asked.

The heavy weight of blankness shifted a little. So she was his mother, was she?

'Yes,' she said.

'You must hurry up and make my breakfast,' he said. 'We get punished if we are late for school.'

'What's today?' she asked.

'It's Friday,' he said. 'I know is Friday because yesterday we had library and library is Thursday.'

The heavy blanket shifted a little more. She hung on to his chatter about the football team. It was called the Big

Sixteen; eight for each side. After he had walked up the dusty brown road to school she struggled into town on the bicycle and returned with the football, a piece of meat and twelve bottles of beer. She drank the beer and sank down to the deep pit of depression. She was supposed to commit suicide at a quarter to one. The depression reached such a stage that by twelve-thirty she stood up and took the tin full of tablets out of the drawer. They were very hard; she would have to melt them down. Just then the voices of several small boys sounded outside the gate. Her son crashed into the house.

'I don't want any lunch,' he said.

And crashed out of the house with the football. They set up a football pitch outside the house. All afternoon she stood at the window watching them. Shorty kicked the ball too high. He fell flat on his back. He stood up, kicked again and fell flat on his back. The pain in her chest was so intense, it was all she could do just to stand at the window and hold on to life. It didn't help either when Tom came around at sunset. She was an aching mass of nerves from head to foot, and the anguish of soul had risen so high that it stood between her and everything. He flung the soiled sweater over the draining board and started to wash his face and arms in the sink.

'How are you?' he asked.

She stood near the sink. She averted her face. She had never been in a position before where one had to admit every day that one was dying. He paused and squinted at her anxiously:

'I have to go away suddenly, and I'll be away for some time,' he said. 'There won't be anyone to take care of you while I'm away.'

How life changed for the ailing! Her only pride was the emotional self-sufficiency of the orphan. It wasn't there now. There had been other times when she had stood near the sink and watched him wash in a storm of laughter and argument. It wasn't him as a person she'd noticed washing but the work they talked about, the living day just past, and a wild and exuberant freedom of heart. It had fallen away. She only noticed the person washing. It was like asking for too much. No other friendship she'd ever had had been so clearly defined. She'd never noticed until then their exactly half and half contribution to it. It was as though he had half the pattern of her mental responses. They used to meet each other half way, throwing ideas to and fro. She wasn't producing that half any longer. He cooked the food again, he talked, but he stood alone. The effort to communicate with her exhausted him. It was strictly a friendship for sound, sane health of mind and body. It wasn't as though he didn't have enough sympathy for her to actually pull him into the whirlpool of darkness but she didn't need anyone there. She preferred to die alone.

'Goodbye,' he said at last. 'I'll see you again, Elizabeth, as soon as I come back.'

Oh, the life-lines he'd thrown her, from a heart so generous it could feed a billion people.

She was afraid to sleep in case she should wake up the next morning alive but without a mind. She sat up half the night. The insects brooded to themselves outside about the summer which was over now and the provisions they had made for winter. Sello kept on saying something. His voice sounded like the brooding insects because he talked so softly. It came to her in snatches:

'Don't hate me, Elizabeth. . . .' Then he seemed to say very carefully: 'I like you.' Then he said: 'All I told you about the times of darkness was true. It affected everything, children and animals. Yes, they misused animals too. . . . But it isn't true that I'm a pervert. Dan cooked it up. . . .'

Just near dawn she dozed off. Instantly Dan arose before her. He said: 'I have the power to take the life of your son. He will be dead in two days.'

She jerked awake and stared with absolute despair at another day. A vague thought was tugging at her mind: Mrs Jones, Mrs Jones. What was it she wanted to say to Mrs Jones? She sat sipping a cup of tea, watching Shorty eat his breakfast. He was eating in a horrible way, shovelling the food roughly into his mouth; he was mad about football and wanted to get out of the house. It was Saturday. There was no school.

'Take a note to Mrs Jones for me,' she said.

'What do you want to say?' he asked.

'Shut up,' she said. 'Just take the note. I can't stand the way you eat food.'

'Dear Mrs Jones,' she wrote. 'I'm sorry I hit you. I've lived in a nightmare world of no compassion for three years.'

Shorty had hardly gone out of the house when Mrs Jones came shuffling down the small brown road. She stumbled into the house and looked at Elizabeth with wide hurt eyes which were full of suppressed tears. There was too much for her to say. She sat down and started with her favourite platitude:

'I kept on wanting to come and visit you, Elizabeth,' she said. 'But I was afraid to upset you.'

She stared at Elizabeth very earnestly, then burst out:

'You must not be afraid of evil. Jesus overcame evil a long time ago.'

'Yes,' Sello said so loudly that Elizabeth jumped.

The old woman appeared not to have heard him. She was sitting right opposite him, and he was staring at her intently. Most probably she thought Elizabeth had said it.

'I simply put my trust in Jesus,' she said. 'I said to him: "Lord, take my life for your service. Use me as you see fit. I know I haven't much. I'm not a wonderful person. But I like to help you, Lord. I do everything you tell me to. When people are lonely, I visit them. When people are sick, I visit them." You mustn't worry about evil like that, Elizabeth.'

Elizabeth stared back at her in disbelief. There was something on her face she had not seen for a long time; the normal, the human, the friendly soft kind glow about the eyes.

'I cannot seem to absorb anything now,' Elizabeth said. 'My heart and mind are dead, as though they are not really there.'

'It's all right,' Mrs Jones said. 'I'll pray for you . . .' And she rambled off into one of her long soliloquies which usually made her drowsy. Elizabeth was not really listening. She was looking at the human being.

Elizabeth thought: 'When people pray: "Oh, God help me", they are praying to something they have in mind that is consistently tender, a concept of goodness that is almost feminine in its pity and mercy. But they generally walk around looking like this God they are praying to. Most people have her expression; a softness, a vague unplannedness, a helplessness, a childlike pity and appeal. Then who are they praying to? Surely they are praying to a God they will never see, because there is no God like ordinary people. You'll find Medusa and Dan in heaven and hell, but you won't find ordinary human kindness and decency there. God in heaven is too important to be decent . . .'

Mrs Jones was asking her a question. She struggled to bring her mind into focus on what she was saying. Mrs Jones stood up. She said: 'If you show me where you keep the things, I'll make the tea. Don't you worry. You just sit down. You look so poorly.'

Elizabeth sat back. Nothing was the same. She'd been suffering before, but she'd still enjoyed tea with Mrs Jones. The hazy nightmare of eternal darkness had completely enclosed her life.

She had spent many week-ends like that; watching Dan gyrate with the nice-time girls. The show was frantic; the women seemed to be doing their finale; they were prancing around stark naked. She kept on going under with beer and tablets. On the Monday morning she jerked into life screaming in silent terror. Shorty had a high fever. Dan said he would be dead in two days' time. She rushed him to hospital. It was only a bruise on his knee that had festered and caused the fever. She came home and put him to bed and lay down. He fell fast asleep, with an Aspro.

All day long she lay down, feeling her life ebb out of her. In the feverish approach of death she heard Dan announce that he was going to go with B. . . . The Womb. He was saying she had a womb he could not forget. They were going and going, frenziedly. She half raised herself from the bed. It was just getting dark. She wanted a cup of tea.

Sello said: 'Oh, I've never seen such savage cruelty!'

She turned her head towards her son's room, and Sello added: 'Elizabeth, love isn't like that. Love is two people mutually feeding each other, not one living on the soul of the other like a ghoul!'

The words sank deep into her battered mind. She repeated

them again. She stood up and made tea and gave Shorty some porridge. Something was giving way. The pain in her chest subsided. The storm in her head subsided. She actually felt a sensation of being lifted and flung clear out of purgatory. In one jubilant shout of joy she swung around to Sello with outstretched hands: 'Thank you! Oh God, thank you for the lever out of hell.'

Things happened quickly after that. Sello, the soaring sky-bird, rose, but this time he came walking towards her drenched from head to toe in light. Dan was still going on her bed with The Womb. He looked up at Sello with black, shocked eyes. For a split second he forgot he was God. He scrambled to his feet. He looked like one of those Afrikaner Boers in South Africa who had been caught contravening the Immorality Act with a black woman. Sello only looked at him from a great height and said nothing.

Dan recovered himself. He spat at Sello:

'I'm not going to be a part of your shit!'

He turned and looked at Elizabeth with deadly hatred:

'I hated you,' he said. 'I'm going to pursue you until I destroy you.'

He walked out, slamming the door hard. The Womb was so terror-stricken at this unexpected turn of events that she dropped to the ground and crawled out of the house, trembling from end to end.

'Who is he?' Elizabeth asked.

'Satan,' Sello said.

Sello walked to the window and looked out at the dark Motabeng night. He talked softly, the way one does after a terrible storm because the heart is appalled.

'I'm sorry,' he said. 'I'm sorry for all that's happened. It was a battle of wits, my brains against his, and he was as treacherous and slippery as a cobra. I had to turn him into a damp squib. That red fire you saw; it's always been a trouble-spot. It maddens the man in possession of it. It's blown up civilization after civilization, and he had acquired enough of it to shatter the whole universe. I saw into him some time ago. I woke him up and made him feel the whole impact of it. He rocked. He went mad. He saw that he could break and bend all life to his will. He was passive, watching everything.

The only miscalculation he made was you. The moment they take on battle with you, they're dead before they know they are. You still topple giants with a stone sling.'

He turned and smiled affectionately at Elizabeth.

'There are so many layers of awareness,' he continued. 'I showed him your surface layer, the perfection of your service to mankind. Bring an inferior into contact with a superior; he jumps on you and tramples you into the dust. He saw only what he thought was the milksop monk; it was so soft and tender it aroused all his savage, brutal passions. They go wild when they see something helpless, defenceless. They never attack something their own size. I never showed him the terrible power behind the milksop monk. I operated it in the background, to kill him. We've taken away the major danger, because that power combined with his will to evil could create such darkness it would be oblivion. That's what they were all like before the time of darkness, or, as it is said, the fall of man. They saw their powers and killed, mercilessly. There's nothing I can do about the filth of his mind and heart, but I saw a way of taking away his power, through you. You were created with ten billion times more power than he. It was done at a time of desperation, and our weapon of war against the power-maniacs was concealed behind the facade of a laughing clown. You will never know your power. I will never let you see it because I know what power does. *If the things of the soul are really a question of power, then anyone in possession of power of the spirit could be Lucifer.*'

He paused and brooded.

'It wasn't power that was my doom. It was women; in particular a special woman who formed a creative complement to me, much like the relationship you and I have had for some time. She was captivating and dazzling. I liked slaves. I could never say goodbye. I could never accept a rejection. I was too important. I tried to break her. She had your power. She broke free and unleashed centuries of suffering and darkness. Nothing stood in the way of her prestige and self-esteem; she was God. She was like Dan with a terrible will, with magic rituals and all kinds of tricks. I saw the story repeating itself because, once he saw his power, he wanted to be God on the strength of his power, irrespective of the fact that his heart is filth. What he showed you was all that he had in his heart. There was nothing else. He saw the opposite in you. He saw the monk. He thought you might not fall in with his plans. That's why he took you on, to remould you in his own image. I gave him a free hand because I wanted to study, completely, his image. And I thought you needed the insight into absolute evil. I'm sorry it was so painful.'

He paused and looked at her with an anguished expression:

'I gained an insight into everything, right from the start. Since I dominated the situation, I thought all the wrong things. What would you do, once you know everything and there is a lot to hide?'

That was the crux of it, once she knew and was certain of the truth, she would disclose it, no matter if it was the most horrific truth mankind had ever heard. But in spite of those three or four years of sustained nightmare, she really knew absolutely nothing, except that she had gained an insight into what the German concentration camps must have been like. The inmates had cried: 'Oh Lord, where are you?' No Lord had appeared to help them. No Lord ever would. She had no illusions left about God or mercy or pity. A victim simply stared in the face of evil, and died. Sello knew that and if there was a truth to be disclosed about the world of the soul, he had to disclose it. She had no reply.

He looked out of the window and said, impersonally:

'Thank you for all you've done. Our friendship will never end.'

He frightened her deeply. He'd conducted a strange drama, in a secret way, and it had been so terrible that she had gone insane. He'd also, according to Dan, included her in his prophecies, which endangered human life because they aroused jealousy; a prophet must be a freak, something special and apart from the rest of mankind, someone who produced the wine from water, and she couldn't do any of that. She felt as normal and ordinary as other people, yet she had nearly been killed in this rigmarole of hell. Funny thing, though, she really adored Sello, as though they were two companions who shared a permanent joke.

'Sello,' she said. 'If you say our friendship will never end, that means we are supposed to meet again in other lives?'

'Yes,' he said.

'Would you like to be my brother?'

'All right,' he said.

'I'll look around for suitable parents for us,' she said, cunningly. 'I'm much better than you at organizing family affairs, and once I find the parents you will always be my favourite brother.'

She simply meant she wanted parents who did not believe in prophecies. They boiled down to bugger all, and they made a normal happy person, who loved birds, insects, vegetable gardens and people, the victim of Dan.

He was laughing. Didn't one laugh when torture and evil became irrelevant? But, more than that, Sello had the heart of the wild gambler. He was always out somewhere spinning coins. He showed her a travelling bag. When he opened it, she saw that it was filled with an incandescent light.

'It's the message of the brotherhood of man,' he said.

She left the story like that, unresolved. She only recorded the one-sided view of her own observations and speculations. The rest of it was in the hands of Sello. He had the long history of the human race in his heart, as he was Old Father Time. Whatever would happen next she could not say, because her mind retreated to its own privacy. A slow, upwelling joy and happiness made her feel that the future might be simpler and more beautiful than the crookery of Dan.

Sello took a photograph out of his pocket. It was the picture of him and his girl walking down a road, hand in hand.

'You have my wife,' he said.

The wife of Buddha emerged from Elizabeth's person and walked towards Sello. She quietly settled herself at his feet. She was a queen of heaven who was a housekeeper. She'd travelled a journey with a man who had always deserted her in a pursuit after the things of the soul. He'd achieved his Nirvana and she'd toppled him out of it, she'd stained his hands with blood. Maybe the world would be a little saner, after the strains of the past were over and women were both goddesses and housekeepers and there was a time for loving.

Maybe, the work she and Sello had done together had introduced a softness and tenderness into mankind's history. The flowers, the animals, the everyday events of people's lives had been exalted by them. They had roamed the world together as barefoot monks, and eaten strange food to sustain them through their monastic disciplines. No lover had caressed them in their solitary meditations on the soul, yet they had been lovers of mankind. She struck at the spring of it, the source of it, that night. They had perfected together the ideal of sharing everything and then perfectly shared everything with all mankind.

To rediscover that love was like suddenly being transported to a super-state of life. It was the point at which all personal love had died in them. It was the point at which there were no private hungers to be kissed, loved, adored. And yet there was a feeling of being kissed by everything; by the air, the soft flow of life, people's smiles and friendships; and, propelled forward by the acquisition of this vast and universal love, they had moved among men again and again and told them they loved them. That was the essential nature of their love for each other. It had included all mankind, and so many things could be said about it, but the most important was that it equalized all things and all men.

David's song arose in her heart once more, but this time infinitely more powerful and secure: 'I have been through the valley of the shadow of death, but I fear no evil. I shall dwell in the house of the Lord forever.' She treasured the encounter with Dan. The suffering she had endured had sealed her Achille's heel; that of the brutal murderer for love. And she'd told Medusa that she was retracing the pathway to the achievement of Buddha. But Dan had blasted her to a height far above Buddha; he had deepened and intensified all her qualities. He was one of the greatest teachers she'd worked with, but he taught by default – he taught iron and steel self-control through sheer, wild, abandoned debauchery; he taught the extremes of love and tenderness through the extremes of hate; he taught an alertness for falsehoods within, because he had used any means at his disposal to destroy Sello. And from the degradation and destruction of her life had arisen a still, lofty serenity of soul nothing could shake.

Towards dawn she threw the packet of tablets out of the window.

Elizabeth could never do anything normally. She had a permanently giddy head. She had reeled towards death. She turned and reeled towards life. She reeled, blissfully happy, up the dusty brown road, down the pathway into the valley area of the local-industries project. She paused at the garden gate. Kenosi stood on a trench-bed upturning the soil with a fork. A small boy was watering. A man was preparing a new trench-bed.

'Kenosi!' she shouted, jubilantly.

Kenosi immediately dropped the fork and came walking towards her, nod, nod, nodding her cat's head. They met half way in the middle of the garden. She stopped and stared at Elizabeth severely.

'Dumela,' she said, quietly.

'I have been ill,' Elizabeth said.

'Eugene told me,' she said. 'He was very worried.'

'I've come back to work,' Elizabeth said. 'Let me see the garden.'

They began walking down Main Street or Broadway. Suddenly Kenosi raised her voice and said plaintively:

'You left the garden. I don't know how to do. We became poor. When you were here we used to make R4.00 every week from vegetables; R4.00 from gooseberry jam. No one could do jam. The vegetables came down to R2.00.'

She pulled out of her pocket the garden record book of vegetable sales and handed it to Elizabeth. There in a shaky, painstaking handwriting was a meticulous record of all she had sold. The spelling, oh, the spelling was a fantastic combination of English and Setswana:

'Ditamati 30c,' she wrote. 'Pamkin 6oc, Dibeetteruti 45c, Dionions 25c, Dibeans 20c, Dispinach 15c, Dicarrots 25c, Ditamati 45c. . . .'

Elizabeth laughed silently. That garden was hallowed ground to Kenosi. She could see her over those months sitting at a table in her hut at night with a candle, frowning over all the entries she made, careful not to lose a cent. The record book looked so beautiful that Elizabeth kept quietly turning it over in her head – Ditamati, Dionions, Dispinach, Dibeans, Dicarrots – as she and Kenosi walked up and down the garden. Kenosi said they had no tomato seedlings and they needed more cabbage and she hadn't been able to buy seed potato. She watched with pride as Elizabeth made a note of all the garden requirements. Whatever they needed, Elizabeth had always found by hook or crook. They began to think together again. Tomorrow they would plant out more carrots and beetroot; there'd be time today for seedling work. And so the morning flew by. The world had returned to normal again. The strained look left Kenosi's face. Elizabeth had once read a story about a cat called Jackson. His full name was Hold-The-Fort-For-I'm-Coming-Jackson. Cats are normally cool creatures. Kenosi sighed over and over; so many things had gone wrong in the fort while the commander was out on the battlefield slaying the devil. They filled seedlings bags, they talked about gooseberry jam – there were thousands and thousands of gooseberries under the trees in Elizabeth's yard. They'd kept on falling while she was away and no one had picked them. Kenosi sighed richly. They had ahead of them an income in a week or two of R10 from gooseberry jam alone. At midday they stood up together and walked back to Elizabeth's house. They'd have lunch and pick gooseberries and start some of the jam-making in the afternoon. Along the pathway they met the Eugene man. He stopped and stared at Elizabeth. What could she say? He'd always helped her and things kept going wrong. Then she'd beaten Mrs Jones too. She started to say something about having made a terrible mess and hurt people. He cut her short, raised his head proudly and said: 'You'll make up for it.' He was that kind of man. People were always going up and up and up, never down and down and down.

At sunset, when work was over and everything was peaceful, slowly sipping a cup of tea, she began to jot down fragmentary notes such as a shipwrecked sailor might make on a warm sandy beach as he stared back at the stormy sea that had nearly taken his life. At first nothing of her own would come to her. A D. H. Lawrence poem – *Song Of A Man Who Has Come Through* – kept on welling up in her mind: 'Not I, but the wind that blows through me! A fine wind is blowing the new direction of time. If only I let it bear me. . . . If only, most lovely of all, I yield myself and am borrowed by the fine wind that takes its course through the chaos of the world. . . . Oh, for the wonder that bubbles into my soul . . .'

Then Shorty crept into the house.

'Hello, darling,' she said, absent-mindedly.

'Hello, darling,' he said. 'What are you doing?'

'I'm writing poetry,' she said.

'I know about that,' he said. 'I learned about it in school. I can write a poem too.'

Vaguely she noticed that his face had become a flame of concentration. Amused, she noticed that he imitated her. He stopped to sip his tea, then write. He asked her to spell butterfly and honey. The darkness fell upon them, and still they sat dreaming in the light of two candles on the table. Then he handed her his poem. She had to read it through several times in disbelief. It seemed impossible that he had really travelled the journey alongside her. He seemed to summarize all her observations.

> *The man,* he wrote. *The man*
> *Can fly about the sky,*
> *Sky butterflies can fly,*
> *Bees can make honey,*
> *And what else can fly?*
> *Sky birds, sky aeroplanes, sky helicopters,*
> *Sky jets, sky boeings can fly,*
> *A fairy man and a fairy boy*
> *Can fly about the sky.*

That's what she felt about people's souls and their powers; that they were like sky birds, aeroplanes, jets, boeings, fairies and butterflies; that there'd be a kind of liberation of these powers, and a new dawn and a new world. She felt this because the basic error seemed to be a relegation of all things holy to some unseen Being in the sky. Since man was not holy to man, he could be tortured for his complexion, he could be misused, degraded and killed. If there were any revelation whatsoever in her own suffering it seemed to be quite the reverse of Mohammed's dramatic statement. He had said: There is only one God and his name is Allah. And Mohammed is his prophet.

She said: There is only one God and his name is Man. And Elizabeth is his prophet.

These themes of thought clung about her. A peaceful, meditative privacy settled on her mind. Her painful, broken nerve-ends quietly knit together. She put Shorty to bed and, for the first time in three years, embraced the solitude of the night with joy.

The elegant pathway of private thought stretched ahead of her, shimmering with light and undisturbed by the clamour of horrors. She turned and picked up a book from a table beside her bed. It had waited for a whole year to be read. It was: *The Gift Of A Cow*, by Premchand. It was a UNESCO publication of the classic Hindi novel which exalted the poor. In their introduction to the novel they wrote that it opposed the basic trend of Indian literature, which seemed to be a literature intended only 'to entertain and to satisfy our lust for the amazing . . .' a literature of magic, of ghosts, of the adventures of high-born heroes and heroines.

It was quite the opposite in Africa. There was no direct push against those rigid, false social systems of class and caste. She had fallen from the very beginning into the warm embrace of the brotherhood of man, because when a people wanted everyone to be ordinary it was just another way of saying man loved man. As she fell asleep, she placed one soft hand over her land. It was a gesture of belonging.

THE AFRICAN WRITERS SERIES

SYL CHENEY-COKER
The Last Harmattan of Alusine Dunbar

The first novel of this well-known poet tells the story of a Sierra Leone-like country and its pioneers seeking freedom after the American Revolution.

NADINE GORDIMER
Crimes of Conscience

A selection of short stories which vividly describe human conditions and the turmoil of a violent world outside the individual incidents, where the instability of fear and uncertainty lead unwittingly to crimes of conscience.

NGŨGĨ
Matigari

This is a moral fable telling the story of a freedom fighter and his quest for Truth and Justice. It is set in the political dawn of post-independence Kenya.
'Clear, subtle, mischievous, passionate novel'. *Sunday Times*

AMECHI AKWANYA
Orimili

Set in a complex Nigerian Community that's at the point of irrevocable change, this is the story of a man's struggle to be accepted in the company of his town's elders.

SHIMMER CHINODYA
Harvest of Thorns

'Zimbabwe has fine black writers and Shimmer Chinodya is one of the best. *Harvest of Thorns* brilliantly pictures the transition between the old, white-dominated Southern Rhodesia, through the Bush War, to the new black regime. It is a brave book, a good strong story, and it is often very funny. People who know the country will salute its honesty, but I hope newcomers to African writing will give this book a try. They won't be disappointed.' Doris Lessing

CHINUA ACHEBE
Things Fall Apart

This, the first title in the African Writers Series, describes how a man in the Igbo tribe of Nigeria became exiled from the tribe and returned only to be forced to commit suicide to escape the results of his rash courage against the white man.